The Church at Worship: Case Studies from Christian History

Series Editors: Lester Ruth, Carrie Steenwyk, John D. Witvliet

Longing

for Jesus

Worship at a Black Holiness Church in Mississippi, 1895–1913

LESTER RUTH

William B. Eerdmans Publishing Company

Grand Rapids, Michigan / Cambridge, U.K.

Published 2013 by

WM. B. EERDMANS PUBLISHING CO.

2140 Oak Industrial Drive N.E., Grand Rapids, Michigan 49505 /

P.O. Box 163, Cambridge CB3 9PU U.K.

Printed in the United States of America

18 17 16 15 14 13   7 6 5 4 3 2 1

Library of Congress Cataloging-in-Publication Data

Ruth, Lester, 1959–

   Longing for Jesus : worship at a black holiness church in Mississippi, 1895-1913 / Lester Ruth.

      pages   cm. — (The church at worship : case studies from Christian history)

   Includes bibliographical references and index.

   ISBN 978-0-8028-6949-4 (pbk. : alk. paper)

1. Christ Temple (Jackson, Miss.) — History. 2. Church of Christ (Holiness) U.S.A. — Case studies.

3. Church of Christ (Holiness) U.S.A. — History. 4. African Americans — Religion.

5. Public worship. 6. Holiness churches — History. 7. Black churches — History.

8. Jones, Charles Price, 1865-1949. 9. Jackson (Miss.) — Church history.   I. Title.

   BX7012.Z7J33   2013

   289.9 — dc23

                                        2013009742

www.eerdmans.com

Contents

PART THREE: ASSISTING THE INVESTIGATION

Series Introduction

The Church at Worship offers user-friendly documentary case studies in the history of Christian worship. The series features a wide variety of examples, both prominent and obscure, from a range of continents, centuries, and Christian traditions. Whereas many historical studies of worship survey developments over time, offering readers a changing panoramic view like that offered out of an airplane window, each volume in *The Church at Worship* zooms in close to the surface, lingering over worship practices in a single time and place and allowing readers to sense the texture of specific worship practices in unique Christian communities. To complement books that study "the forest" of liturgical history, these volumes study "trees in the forest."

Each volume opens by orienting readers to the larger contexts of each example through a map, a timeline of events, and a summary of significant aspects of worship in the relevant time period and region. This section also includes any necessary cautions for the study of the particular case, as well as significant themes or practices to watch for while reading.

Each volume continues by focusing on the practices of worship in the specific case. This section begins with an introduction that explains the nature of participation in worship for ordinary worshipers. Many studies of worship have focused almost exclusively on what clergy do, say, and think. In contrast, insofar as historical sources allow it, this series focuses on the nature of participation of the entire community.

Each volume next presents an anthology of primary sources, presenting material according to the following categories: people and artifacts, worship setting and space, descriptions of worship, orders of service and texts, sermons, polity documents, and theology-of-worship documents. Each source is introduced briefly and is accompanied by a series of explanatory notes. Inclusion of these primary sources allows readers to have direct access to the primary material that historians draw upon for their summary descriptions and comparisons of practices. These sources are presented in ways that honor both academic rigor and accessibility. Our aim is to provide the best English editions of the resources possible, along with a complete set of citations that allow researchers to find quickly the best scholarly editions. At the same time, the introductory comments, explanatory sidebars, detailed glossaries, and devotional and small-group study questions make these volumes helpful not only for scholars and students but also for congregational study groups and a variety of other interested readers.

The presentation of sources attempts, insofar as it is possible, to take into account multiple disciplines of study related to worship. Worship is inevitably a multi-sensory experience, shaped by the sounds of words and music, the sight of symbols and spaces, the taste of bread and wine, and the fragrance of particular places and objects. Worship is also shaped by a variety of sources that never appear in the event itself: scriptural commands, theological treatises, and church polity rules or guidelines. In order to help readers sense this complex interplay, the volumes in this series provide a wide variety of texts and images. We particularly hope that this approach helps students of the history of preaching, architecture, and music, among others, to more deeply understand how their interests intersect with other disciplines.

Each volume concludes with suggestions for devotional use, study questions for congregational study groups, notes for students working in a variety of complementary disciplines, a glossary, suggestions for further study, works cited, and an index.

Students of Christian worship, church history, religious studies, and social or cultural history might use these case studies to complement the bird's-eye view offered by traditional textbook surveys.

Students in more specialized disciplines — including both liberal arts humanities (e.g., architectural or music history) and the subdisciplines of practical theology (e.g., evangelism, preaching, education, and pastoral care) — may use these volumes to discern how their own topic of interest interacts with worship practices. Liturgical music, church architecture, and preaching, for example, cannot be fully understood apart from a larger context of related practices.

This series is also written for congregational study groups, adult education classes, and personal study. It may be unconventional in some contexts to plan a congregational study group around original historical documents. But there is much to commend this approach. A reflective encounter with the texture of local practices in other times and places can be a profound act of discipleship. In the words of Andrew Walls, "Never before has the Church looked so much like the great multitude whom no one can number out of every nation and tribe and people and tongue. Never before, therefore, has there been so much potentiality for mutual enrichment and self-criticism, as God causes yet more light and truth to break forth from his word."[1]

This enrichment and self-criticism happens, in part, by comparing and contrasting the practices of another community with our own. As Rowan Williams explains, "Good history makes us think again about the definition of things we thought we understood pretty well, because it engages not just with what is familiar but with what is strange. It recognizes that 'the past is a foreign country' as well as being *our* past."[2] This is possible, in part, because of a theological conviction. As Williams points out, ". . . there is a sameness in the work of

---

1. Andrew Walls, *The Missionary Movement in Christian History: Studies in the Transmission of Faith* (Maryknoll, N.Y.: Orbis Books, 1996), p. 15.
2. Rowan Williams, *Why Study the Past? The Quest for the Historical Church* (Grand Rapids: Wm. B. Eerdmans, 2005), p. 1.

God. . . . We are not the first to walk this way; run your hand down the wood and the grain is still the same."[3] This approach turns on its head the minimalist perspective that "those who cannot remember the past are condemned to repeat it."[4] That oft-repeated truism implies that the goal of studying history is merely to avoid its mistakes. A more robust Christian sensibility is built around the conviction that the past is not just a comedy of errors but the arena in which God has acted graciously.

We pray that as you linger over this and other case studies in this series, you will be challenged and blessed through your encounter with one small part of the very large family of God. Near the end of his magisterial volume *A Secular Age,* Charles Taylor concludes, "None of us could ever grasp alone everything that is involved in our alienation from God and his action to bring us back. But there are a great many of us, scattered through history, who have had some powerful sense of some facet of this drama. Together we can live it more fully than any one of us could alone." What might this mean? For Taylor it means this: "Instead of reaching immediately for the weapons of polemic, we might better listen for a voice which we could never have assumed ourselves, whose tone might have been forever unknown to us if we hadn't *strained to understand it.* . . ."[5] We hope and pray that readers, eager to learn from worship communities across time and space, will indeed strain to understand what they find in these studies.

LESTER RUTH
Duke Divinity School
The Robert E. Webber Institute for Worship Studies

CARRIE STEENWYK
Calvin Institute of Christian Worship
Calvin College and Calvin Theological Seminary

JOHN D. WITVLIET
Calvin Institute of Christian Worship
Calvin College and Calvin Theological Seminary

---

3. Williams, *Why Study the Past?* p. 29.
4. George Santayana, *The Life of Reason* (New York: Scribner's, 1905), p. 284.
5. Charles Taylor, *A Secular Age* (Cambridge: Harvard University Press, 2007), p. 754.

Suggestions for Complementary Reading

For students of Christian worship wanting to survey the broader landscape, we recommend using the examples of these volumes alongside other books such as Geoffrey Wainwright and Karen B. Westerfield Tucker's *Oxford History of Christian Worship* (Oxford University Press, 2005); Gail Ramshaw's *Christian Worship: 100,000 Sundays of Symbols and Rituals* (Fortress Press, 2009); Marcel Metzger's *History of the Liturgy: The Major Stages,* translated by Madeleine Beaumont (Collegeville, MN: Liturgical Press 1997); Frank C. Senn's *The People's Work: A Social History of the Liturgy* (Fortress Press, 2006) and *Christian Liturgy: Catholic and Evangelical* (Fortress Press, 1997); and James F. White's *Introduction to Christian Worship* (Abingdon Press, 2001), *A Brief History of Christian Worship (*Abingdon Press, 1993), and *Protestant Worship* (Westminster John Knox Press, 2006).

For those studying church history, volumes from this series might accompany volumes such as Mark Noll's *Turning Points: Decisive Moments in the History of Christianity* (Baker Academic, 2001) and Justo Gonzalez's *Church History: An Essential Guide* (Abingdon Press, 1996) and *The Story of Christianity,* vols. 1-2 (HarperOne, 1984 and 1985).

Students of religious studies might read these volumes alonside Robert A. Segal's *The Blackwell Companion to the Study of Religion* (Wiley-Blackwell, 2008) and John R. Hinnell's *The Routledge Companion to the Study of Religion* (Routledge, 2005).

History of music classes might explore the case studies of this series with Paul Westermeyer's *Te Deum: The Church and Music* (Augsburg Fortress Publishers, 1998) or Andrew Wilson-Dickson's *The Story of Christian Music: From Gregorian Chant to Black Gospel* (Augsburg Fortress Publishers, 2003).

History of preaching students might study the contextual examples provided in this series along with Hughes Oliphant Old's volumes of *The Reading and Preaching of the Scriptures in the Worship of the Christian Church* (Eerdmans, 1998-2007) or O. C. Edwards's *A History of Preaching* (Abingdon Press, 2004).

Acknowledgments

I am grateful to the many people who helped make this volume possible:

to Dr. James Abbington of Candler School of Theology and Mrs. Anita Jefferson, a long-time Church of Christ (Holiness) U.S.A. member and historian. At the beginning of the journey and along the way, both have been indispensable in resourcing and shaping this volume;

to the members and leaders within the Church of Christ (Holiness) U.S.A. Thanks especially to Bishop Emery Lindsay, Bishop Victor Smith, Bishop Dale Cudjoe, Euel and Alberta Bunton, and Willie Taylor. I appreciate, too, the warm welcome the congregation at Christ Temple gave me when I visited;

to people affiliated with Mt. Helm Baptist Church. I offer thanks to Levernis Crosby, Rev. C. J. Rhodes, and Dr. Lee E. Williams Jr.;

to Dr. John Giggie, Dr. Dale Irvin, Dr. David Douglas Daniels, Dr. Eric Washington, and Willingham Castilla for their invaluable assistance;

to Angela Stewart, archivist at the Archive and Museum of the African-American Experience in the Margaret Walker Center of Jackson State University, for her bibliographic help;

to Lee Rider for taking time out of his busy ministry schedule to visit the Mississippi State Archives on my behalf;

to Rachel Adams, Calvin Brondyke, Samantha Brondyke, Kyle Erffmeyer, Matt Gritter, Kent Hendricks, Shelley Veenstra Hendricks, Courtney Hexham, Rachel Klompmaker, Jana Kelder Koh, Brenda Janssen Kuyper, Anneke Leunk, Asher Mains, Becky Boender Ochsner, Kendra Pennings, Katie Roelofs, Katie Ritsema Roelofs, Eric Rottman, Annica Vander Linde, Bethany Meyer Vrieland, Tracie VerMerris Wiersma, Joanna Kooyenga Wigboldy, and Eric Zoodsma, whose work at the Calvin Institute of Christian Worship as student assistants has included hours of copying, scanning, typing and other support for this volume;

to my editorial comrades, Carrie Steenwyk and John Witvliet, for making this volume possible;

to the Lilly Endowment for financial support;

and to Mary Hietbrink and Tracey Gebbia for assistance in the publication process.

To any who should be on this list but have been inadvertently left off, I offer both thanks and apologies.

PART ONE

LOCATING THE WORSHIPING COMMUNITY

The Context of the Worshiping Community: Christ Temple, a Black Holiness Church in Jackson, Mississippi, Early Twentieth Century

At the start of the twentieth century, a city cemetery sat across the street from **Christ Tabernacle** (or Temple),[1] a new church in Jackson, Mississippi. The juxtaposition of the two could not have been more ironic. On one side of the street lay the resting bodies of governors, mayors, and Confederate soldiers and generals, scattered among the corpses of other notables and average citizens. On the other side of the street rose the church of one of the most vibrant, dynamic black congregations in Mississippi, if not in the whole South. One side of the street emanated repose; the other, a spreading spiritual vitality from a church led by one of the rising stars of the post–Civil War, African-American world, an impressive preacher and songwriter named Charles Price (or C. P.) Jones.

With Jones at the helm, Christ Tabernacle was working hard to worship God in a way true to the Bible and true to its members. The task of remaining true to its members was a particularly challenging struggle at the time. The church juggled its members' heritage as black Christians, including practices and perceptions that reached back even to the days of slavery, with what it meant to be a public church in tumultuous social and religious times. It was a church whose members and pastors were trying to carve out a niche for themselves as African-American Christians as the Civil War faded, a new century dawned, and **Jim Crow** racism lurked in the shadows. What would the worship of such a congregation be like?

That such a congregation could be started at all was a startling development of the late nineteenth century, dependent upon two major reversals that occurred in America's first hundred years. Christ Temple could not have been imaginable just a few decades previous to its start, not to mention at the start of the nation. Yet as the twentieth century began, an enterprising black pastor could plant a church with vitality and influence felt across the nation.

One reversal that cleared the way for Christ Temple was the American Civil War and the resulting emancipation of slaves. This emancipation and the **Reconstruction** that followed allowed African-American worship to become public with the rise of black churches everywhere. That was not possible prior to the war. A few black congregations had existed, as had a handful of black denominations, mainly in the North.[2] Blacks also worshiped with predominantly white congregations. But a large part of the black worship experience existed in the "invisible institution" — that is, the secret worship lives of slaves. They engaged in their

---

1. The church was sometimes called Christ Tabernacle in its early years.
2. The African Methodist Episcopal Church is an example.

own indigenous form of worship featuring elements that had African, Euro-American, and African-American roots.

With the end of the war in 1865, the black church and its worship gained a more public face, even in the South. New African-American congregations could be formed. And, where black constituencies had already existed in other churches, these groups could separate and begin their own autonomous congregations. What these congregations would look like, who they would identify with, and how they would worship were the pressing questions by the end of the century.

A separation from a white church lay behind Christ Temple's own emergence. It actually split off from a prominent black church, **Mt. Helm Baptist Church**, which itself had separated from Jackson's First Baptist Church, a white congregation that had had a black constituency in it prior to the Civil War. Toward the end of the war, the blacks there were worshiping on their own in the basement, under the leadership of an African-American minister. After the war, the group withdrew from First Baptist Church and built a new facility on land given to them by a white benefactor, Thomas E. Helm, naming the new church after him.

Accepting a call to become the pastor of Mt. Helm Baptist Church in 1895 was what originally brought C. P. Jones to Jackson. Almost thirty years old, educated, and a dynamic speaker, Jones appeared poised to take Mt. Helm to new heights. But the heights were not achieved by Jones, at least not at Mt. Helm. Soon after his arrival, a conflict arose between Jones and some in the congregation. After a contentious lawsuit, which the Jones faction lost, his party was forced to leave and form a separate congregation, which became Christ Temple. The dynamism moved with Jones to this new congregation. In the midst of this drama, what should not be overlooked is the ability of Jones and like-minded African-Americans to plant a new, vibrant black church.

The fact that Jones's churches were Baptist or independent is a sign of the other radical reversal that had occurred in America. The issue is what kind of church Jones pastored. While the nation's Founding Fathers would have been surprised by Jones's ability as a free black man to create a congregation of African-Americans in the capital city of a southern state, they would have been aghast that Jones's church (and most of the churches in that city) did not belong to one of the old-time Protestant churches that had dominated America prior to the Revolution — Anglican (Episcopalian) or Congregational especially. No one in 1776 would have predicted a religious landscape where the key churches in an American city were Baptist, Methodist, or something entirely new.

This shift — what one scholar called the "democratization"[3] of American Christianity — meant that those churches with long traditions of power and influence, led by trained clergy

3. Nathan O. Hatch, *The Democratization of American Christianity* (New Haven: Yale University Press, 1989).

with impeccable credentials, gave way to upstart groups with few markers other than zeal and the Bible. This rise of new churches mirrored the upheaval in democratic political notions of the new nation. In these new churches, authority came from the consent of those who agreed to be led in worship, not from formal indicators of status like tradition and education. Thus Baptist and Methodist denominations and a host of new denominations that were created in the nineteenth century, usually led by preachers who adopted popular expressions of faith, supplanted the churches which previously had formed the center of American religion. At the end of the nineteenth century and the beginning of the twentieth, a new wave of Holiness churches (like Christ Temple) and Pentecostal churches continued this upheaval by threatening to upstage Baptist and Methodist congregations.

Both of these major shifts — the changed social status of America's blacks and the growing prominence of formerly upstart denominations — allowed a talented black minister to start a vibrant congregation which would eventually become the mother church for a new denomination named the Church of Christ (Holiness) U.S.A. Across from the cemetery, something new in religion had been born. Surely some of the dead turned over in their graves.

Timeline

What was happening in the world?	What was happening in Christianity?	What was happening in the Jackson congregation?
	ca. 1850: Landmark Baptist thought, which argues that Baptist churches are the only legitimate churches, emerges.	
1857: The Dred Scott Decision by the U.S. Supreme Court states that a black person cannot be a citizen and thus has no judicial standing in a court.		
1863: President Abraham Lincoln issues the Emancipation Proclamation.		
April 1865: The American Civil War ends with Southern loss.		December 1865: Charles Price Jones is born in Georgia.
December 1865: The abolishment of slavery, the 13th Amendment to the U.S. Constitution, is ratified.		
1865-1877: Reconstruction in the defeated, former Confederate states (including Mississippi) attempts to restore the South.	1867: The National Holiness Association forms in Vineland, New Jersey.	1867: Mt. Helm Baptist Church is formally organized.
July 1868: The guarantee of citizenship to all persons born within the United States, the 14th Amendment to the U.S. Constitution, is ratified. The amendment also obligates states to give due protection of the law to all citizens.	1869: The first black Holiness denomination, the Reformed Zion Union Apostolic Church, is formed.	January 1868: Thomas Helm conveys to the trustees the lots upon which Mt. Helm Baptist Church is built.
February 1870: Another constitutional protection for all citizens is guaranteed by the 15th Amendment, which is ratified. Neither the United States nor any single state can deny rights on the basis of "race, color, or previous condition of servitude."	1870s: Dwight L. Moody (preacher) and Ira Sankey (singer) team up for urban revivals.	1868: The Jackson Baptist Association is formed with 400 members; Rev. Marion Dunbar, pastor of Mt. Helm Baptist Church, is elected first moderator.
1870: Mississippi and Georgia, among the last former Confederate states, are allowed new representation in the U.S. Congress.		
1871: The Mississippi state legislature opens Alcorn University as a college for black men.		
1875: Mark Twain publishes *Tom Sawyer*.	1873: Fanny Crosby writes the hymn "Blessed Assurance."	
ca. 1876: Southern legislatures begin passing Jim Crow laws segregating African-Americans.	1875: Hannah Whitall Smith publishes *The Christian's Secret of a Happy Life*, an important work in the Holiness movement.	

What was happening in the world?	What was happening in Christianity?	What was happening in the Jackson congregation?
1877: The last federal troops are removed from the South.		
1878: Thomas Edison begins serious research into developing the incandescent lightbulb.		
1879: Albert Einstein is born.	1879: The largest Holiness association in America, the Iowa Holiness Association, is formed.	
1880s-1890s: Southern state legislatures enact laws which disenfranchise many black and poor white voters.		1884: Jones is converted.
1884-1885: In Chicago the first skyscraper is built.		1883-1885: Mt. Helm hosts Jackson College after it moves from Natchez, Mississippi. (Jackson College eventually becomes Jackson State University.)
	1887: A. B. Simpson founds the Christian Missionary Alliance. Simpson's teachings and writings are important forerunners of the rise of Pentecostal thought. The Alliance incorporates in 1897.	1888: Jones enters Bible college in Little Rock, Arkansas; he begins a series of pastorates in Baptist churches.
		1888: Jones is ordained by Charles L. Fisher, who would later serve as Mt. Helm's pastor from 1893-1894.
1891: The Confederate Monument on the grounds of the Old Capitol in Jackson is dedicated; the grandson of Jefferson Davis, the president of the Confederacy, does the unveiling.		1891: Jones graduates from Arkansas Bible College.
		1891: Jones encounters the Holiness movement through Joanna Patterson Moore, a white American Baptist missionary.
		1893: Rev. Elbert B. Topp, pastor of Mt. Helm Baptist Church, leaves that church with 210 of its members and starts what will eventually be called Farish Street Baptist Church.
		1893: Jones declines a call to become the pastor of Mt. Helm Baptist Church after holding a preaching revival there after the Topp schism.
1894: The Smith Robertson School, the first public school for African-Americans in Jackson, opens.	1894: The First Baptist Church of Jackson (a white congregation) opens a spacious new building.	1893-1894: Charles L. Fisher serves as pastor of Mt. Helm.
		1894: Jones receives "baptism in the Holy Ghost," which he understands to be the sanctification experience of Holiness movement doctrine.
		1894: Jones again declines a call to become the pastor of Mt. Helm Baptist Church.
		1894-1895: Patrick H. Thompson serves as pastor of Mt. Helm.

What was happening in the world?	What was happening in Christianity?	What was happening in the Jackson congregation?
		1895: Jones accepts the pastorate at Mt. Helm.
1896: In *Plessy v. Ferguson,* the U.S. Supreme Court allows state-mandated segregation through "separate but equal" facilities.	1896: Billy Sunday conducts his first revival.	1896: Jones begins publication of a journal entitled *Truth.*
		1896: Jones organizes the Young Men's Christian League in Jackson.
	1897: Saint Thérèse of Lisieux dies.	June 1897: Jones hosts a Holiness convention at Mt. Helm, a first for that congregation.
		1897: Charles Mason, a comrade in ministry to Jones, organizes the first Holiness congregation in Lexington, Mississippi, after all pulpits are closed to him; this is sometimes considered one of the first Church of God in Christ congregations.
1898: The Spanish-American War occurs.	1898: Campbell College, supported by the African Methodist Episcopal Church, relocates from Vicksburg, Mississippi, to Jackson.	June 1898: Jones and a majority of Mt. Helm members vote to eliminate the name "Baptist" and to be known as the Church of Christ, with no creeds or denominational associations.
		July 1898: The annual session of the General Missionary Baptist Convention of Mississippi condemns the Holiness movement among African-American Baptists. The local Baptist association soon follows suit.
		December 1898: Jones withdraws from the Jackson Baptist Association.
1899: The city of Jackson's trolley system switches from mule-drawn cars to electric cars.	1899: The Gideons International is founded to distribute Scripture.	1899: Jones publishes his first songbook, *Jesus Only,* No. 1.
		February 1899: Mt. Helm Baptist Church begins to rip apart as Jones and a majority of members first vote to change the church's name in the legal records, eliminating their Baptist identity. Approximately 180 people who opposed the name change are removed from membership. Later, under advisement from a lawyer, the majority seek to reverse the name change.
		March 1899: Legal maneuvering starts between different factions at Mt. Helm, with the minority worshiping in a separate building elsewhere in town. Jones retains possession of the original building.

What was happening in the world?

1901: With the assassination of William McKinley, Vice President Theodore Roosevelt becomes president at 42 years old. He serves until 1909.

1903: The Wright brothers fly the first motorized airplane.

1903: Mississippi's new capitol building in Jackson is occupied.

1904: Jackson organizes its first fire department with salaried firemen.

1906: The San Francisco earthquake kills hundreds.

What was happening in Christianity?

1901: Agnes Ozman, one of the students in Charles F. Parham's Bible school in Topeka, Kansas, speaks in tongues after hearing Parham teach from Acts about tongues as the evidence of receiving the Holy Spirit. Parham's teaching and Ozman's experience mark in many ways the rise of Pentecostalism.

1902: Experiencing growth, St. Andrew's Episcopal Church (a white congregation) lays the cornerstone for a new building.

1903: Pope Pius X issues a statement reaffirming the primacy of Gregorian chant for the Mass.

1904: An African-American Seventh-Day Adventist congregation starts in Jackson.

1905: Charles F. Parham starts another Bible school in Houston, Texas. William J. Seymour, a black Holiness evangelist, attends and imbibes Parham's teaching.

1906: William J. Seymour leads the Pentecostal revival in Los Angeles at the Azusa Street Mission. This revival serves as the launching point for many persons' acceptance of Pentecostalism.

1906: The Second Baptist Church of Jackson (a white congregation) has experienced such growth that it constructs a new building at an approximate cost of $22,000.

1907: College Addition Church, an African-American Disciples of Christ congregation, begins in Jackson.

What was happening in the Jackson congregation?

October 1900: A judge in Chancery Court of Hinds County rules for the side associated with C. P. Jones.

1901: Jones publishes his second songbook, *Jesus Only,* Nos. 1 and 2.

October 1901: The Mississippi Supreme Court overturns the lower court's decision.

1902: An expulsion notice forces Jones and loyal parishioners to leave the Mt. Helm building.

1902: Jones publishes *An Appeal to the Sons of Africa,* an anthology to inspire black youth to improve themselves.

1903: The first Christ Temple (or Tabernacle) building is constructed.

1905: A mob burns down the original building.

1906: The second Christ Temple is built at an approximate cost of $16,000; interest and improvements bring the whole sum to an estimated $20,000.

1906: Jones publishes *His Fullness* songbook.

1906 Jones's longtime ministry colleague, Charles H. Mason, along with two other friends, travels to the Azusa Street Pentecostal Revival in Los Angeles. Mason has a Pentecostal experience.

1907: Charles H. Mason, along with two other colleagues of Jones, return from California but can't convince Jones of the propriety of Pentecostalism.

1907: The church's private school moves to a larger campus north of Jackson.

What was happening in the world?

1909: The National Association for the Advancement of Colored People (NAACP) is formed.

1909: William H. Taft assumes the presidency.

1909: Writer Eudora Welty is born in Jackson in a house about 300 yards east of Christ Temple.

1912: The *R.M.S. Titanic* sinks after hitting an iceberg.

1913: The 16th Amendment to the U.S. Constitution allows Congress to collect income taxes.

1914: The Panama Canal opens.

1914-1918: World War I is fought.

1919: The 18th Amendment to the U.S. Constitution establishes the prohibition of alcoholic beverages.

1920: Guaranteeing the right to vote to women, the 19th Amendment to the U.S. Constitution is ratified.

What was happening in Christianity?

1908: Holy Ghost Roman Catholic Church opens as an African-American parish in Jackson.

1910: Chicago Pentecostal pastor William H. Durham causes theological controversy in Pentecostalism by denying the need for a sanctification experience prior to being baptized in the Holy Spirit.

1910: Over one thousand representatives attend the World Missionary Conference, a major ecumenical gathering, in Edinburgh, Scotland.

1910: *The Fundamentals* are published. This series attacks modern biblical criticism and marks the beginnings of fundamentalism.

1910: Mt. Helm Baptist Church rebuilds its building at a cost of $2,400.

1914: The Assemblies of God (eventually the largest Pentecostal denomination) is formed.

1914: Grace Evangelical Lutheran Church starts as an African-American parish in Jackson.

What was happening in the Jackson congregation?

1907: Charles H. Mason separates from Jones and appropriates the name "The Church of God in Christ." Jones and Mason begin two years of legal contention for rights to this name and some property.

1908: The church's private school is chartered as Christ Missionary and Industrial College.

1909: The courts allow Mason and his followers to retain the name "The Church of God in Christ." Mason begins to grow a denomination which will eventually be the largest black Pentecostal church.

1917: Jones starts a new congregation in Los Angeles and shifts most of his ministry there.

1920: Christ Temple and the other churches affiliated with Jones are chartered as The Church of Christ (Holiness) U.S.A.

1927: The Church of Christ (Holiness) U.S.A. adopts an episcopal (bishop-based) form of church government.

1949: C. P. Jones dies.

Liturgical Landscape

What liturgical worlds surrounded Christ Temple? If worshipers at Christ Temple looked around Jackson, Mississippi, at the beginning of the twentieth century, what might they see?

The view would have been overwhelmingly Protestant and mainly **evangelical**. Baptists and Methodists would have predominated in the city, with a sprinkling of churches of other denominations here and there. That wouldn't have meant that the worship was entirely uniform, however. Although the worship within the churches of a single denomination might have had some sort of resemblance across its congregations, diversity occurred for a variety of reasons. The tone and temperament differed, for example, in white and black churches, regardless of denominational label. Other social factors like the economic level of the worshipers and their level of education — not to mention the minister's — contributed to differences in worship, even if the basic framework of actions and texts were the same within churches of the same denomination. Denominations were also marked by uneven growth. At the beginning of the twentieth century, some (but not all) of Jackson's churches were showing increased wealth, stability, and numbers in the post–Civil War era, often evidenced by ambitious building projects. In addition, differences arose between town and country churches, sometimes related to the social and racial factors already mentioned.

The most obvious way to mark the liturgical landscape in Jackson would have been to note the denominational names on church signs. These names reflected liturgical traditions which differed on significant issues. Jackson's Roman Catholics and Episcopalians, for example, belonged to traditions that placed greater weight on frequent administration of the Lord's Supper, had a higher level of ceremony, incorporated symbols like vestments for clergy more widely, followed a more developed yearly calendar, and presumed that worship was led by using a text that was common to the whole tradition. An overview of recent Catholic liturgy can be found by looking at James White's *Roman Catholic Worship: Trent to Today,* 2nd ed. (Collegeville, Minn.: Liturgical Press, 2003). For a general overview of the history of American Christian worship, see Karen B. Westerfield Tucker, "North America," in *The Oxford History of Christian Worship,* ed. Geoffrey Wainwright and Karen B. Westerfield Tucker (New York: Oxford University Press, 2006), pp. 586-632. For a helpful overview of the Episcopal Church as well as others, see James F. White, *Protestant Worship: Traditions in Transition* (Louisville: Westminster John Knox Press, 1989).

In contrast, many of Jackson's other churches would have taken a very different approach to worship: the Lord's Supper would have been much less frequent, although baptism of believers only (usually by immersion) would have been critical; lively congregational singing was important; much less ceremony and traditional symbolism characterized the services; extemporaneous or free-composed prayer was much more important than written texts; and the yearly calendar would have been simpler or perhaps more in tune with Sunday school or secular rhythms. Among the believing groups sharing these broad trends would have been Jackson's Baptists, Pentecostals, Disciples of Christ, and Seventh-Day Adventists. Some of these churches (including some Baptist churches) would have placed emphasis on dramatic experiences of salvation, often accompanied by deeply felt inward transformations and sometimes expressed in outward exuberance. For general histories of Baptist worship, see volume 31 (July 1996) of *Baptist History and Heritage* (which is dedicated to Southern Baptist worship), especially David W. Music, "Baptist Hymnals as Shapers of Worship," pp. 7-17, and James E. Carter, "What Is the Southern Baptist Heritage of Worship?", pp. 38-47. Disciples of Christ were part of the larger **Restoration Movement** that developed in nineteenth-century America. For this group's liturgical history, see Errett Gates, *The Early Relations and Separation of Baptists and Disciples* (Chicago: Christian Century, 1904), and Keith Watkins, *The Breaking of Bread: An Approach to Worship for the Christian Churches* (Nashville: Broadman Press, 1966). Likewise, the Seventh-Day Adventist Church (so named because it worshiped on the seventh day of the week, Saturday, and emphasized the Second Coming of Christ) arose in the latter half of the nineteenth century. See James L. Steven, *Worship among the Pioneers: A Study of the Religious Meetings of the Early Seventh-Day Adventists* (Niles, Mich.: Adventist Heritage Center, 1977). Short statements from many of these groups can be found in *Twenty Centuries of Christian Worship,* ed. Robert E. Webber, vol. 2 of the Complete Library of Christian Worship (Nashville: Star Song, 1994). The manner in which the music and preaching were done sought to lead people to these experiences, in line with the larger phenomenon of evangelical revivalism in America. For a survey of evangelicalism in the late nineteenth century, see David W. Bebbington, *The Dominance of Evangelicalism: The Age of Spurgeon and Moody* (Downers Grove, Ill.: InterVarsity Press, 2005).

Occupying the liturgical middle ground in Jackson would have been the Presbyterian and Methodist churches. While sharing some aspects with the Catholic/Episcopal end of the spectrum (e.g., infant baptism and use of written worship texts), Presbyterians and Methodists also could follow some of the same practices that marked the other kind of churches (e.g., employing extemporaneous prayer and giving a critical role to hearty congregational singing). For a review of Presbyterian worship, see Julius Melton, *Presbyterian Worship in America: Changing Patterns Since 1787* (Richmond: John Knox Press, 1967), and John D. Witvliet, "What America Has Contributed to Reformed Worship," *Reformed Liturgy and Music* 30, no. 3 (1996): 103-111. For a history of American Methodist worship, see Karen B. Westerfield Tucker, *American Methodist Worship* (New York: Oxford University Press, 2000). For a closer look at what happened to Methodism as it became a dominant denomination in the nineteenth century, see A. Gregory Schneider, *The Way of the Cross Leads Home: The Domestication of American Methodism* (Bloomington: Indiana University Press, 1993).

Denominational labels alone would not have been enough to differentiate between Jackson's churches. Worshipers in Jackson would have been aware of the differences that race brought to Sunday mornings so that, regardless of liturgical tradition, churches also shared some characteristics along ethnic lines. Descriptions of the character of black worship — past and present — are available in many places, including *The Black Christian Worship Experience,* ed. Melva Wilson Costen and Darius Leander Swann, revised and enlarged edition, vol. 4 in the Black Church Scholars Series (Atlanta: ITC Press, 1992), and C. Eric Lincoln and Lawrence H. Mamiya, *The Black Church in the African-American Experience* (Durham: Duke University Press, 1990). A good summary of this history can be found in Albert J. Raboteau's *Canaan Land: A Religious History of African Americans* (New York: Oxford University Press, 2001). Readers wanting to hear the voices of a range of black Christians should consult *African American Religious History: A Documentary Witness,* 2nd ed., ed. Milton C. Sernett, the C. Eric Lincoln Series on the Black Experience (Durham: Duke University Press, 1999). Specific materials on black Baptists, the origins for Christ Temple's emergence, can be found in Lora-Ellen McKinney's *Total Praise! An Orientation to Black Baptist Belief and Worship* (Valley Forge, Pa.: Judson Press, 2003) and Walter F. Pitts Jr., *Old Ship of Zion: The Afro-Baptist Ritual in the African Diaspora* (New York: Oxford University Press, 1993).

Jackson worshipers would also have been aware that different socio-economic groups might worship in a different manner, even within the same liturgical tradition and even within the same race or ethnicity. For an examination of this phenomenon among African-Americans in an urban context, see Vattel Elbert Daniel, "Ritual and Stratification in Chicago Negro Churches," *American Sociological Review* 7 (1942): 352-61. Of course, one's socio-economic status can influence one's decision of which church to join. Similarly, a worshiper in Jackson was probably aware of the differences between country and town churches. The outward intensity of emotional exuberance could have been seen along both racial and socio-economic lines to some extent.

Finally, worshipers at Christ Temple would have been aware of churches, including their own, that had come under the influence of the Holiness movement, what pastor C. P. Jones once called "evangelical Christians believing in the higher life in Christ." Rooted in longtime Methodist spirituality and seeking to be a renewal movement that emphasized the saving power of Christ through the Holy Spirit to sanctify a person radically, some strands of the Holiness movement — including the strand preached by Jones — also brought some distinctive worship practices like faith healing. This practice naturally extended the Holiness doctrine of instantaneous sanctification by means of Christ's atoning death to the area of physical illness. Christ Temple's worshipers would have been quite aware of their own distinctiveness as well as those churches newly formed by Jones and his comrades in ministry to be "higher life" churches. Indeed, from 1897 onward, this church hosted an annual "Holiness Conference," which would have showcased the beliefs and practices of the African-American take on the Holiness movement.

After 1906 they would also have been aware of these Holiness emphases coalescing into Pentecostalism, with the addition of speaking in tongues as evidence of being baptized with the Holy Spirit. After that time, they saw many of the former Holiness congregations with which they would have been loosely affiliated — as well as other Holiness bodies in the South — adopt Pentecostal tongues (to the consternation of C. P. Jones and Christ Temple). For a description of the Holiness movement and its relationship to early Pentecostalism, one can turn to Donald W. Dayton, *Theological Roots of Pentecostalism* (Peabody, Mass.: Hendrickson Publishers, 1987), Vinson Synan, *The Holiness-Pentecostal Tradition: Charismatic Movements in the Twentieth Century* (Grand Rapids: Wm. B. Eerdmans, 1997), and *Portraits of a Generation: Early Pentecostal Leaders,* ed. James R. Goff Jr. and Grant Wacker (Fayetteville: University of Arkansas Press, 2002). To examine the African-American facet of this connection more closely, see Leonard Lovett, "Black Holiness Pentecostalism," in *The New International Dictionary of Pentecostal and Charismatic Movements,* rev. ed., ed. Stanley M. Burgess (Grand Rapids: Zondervan, 2002).

Geographical Landscape

This map shows Jackson, Mississippi, around 1920; the block on which Christ Temple and Mt. Helm Baptist stood is highlighted in black.

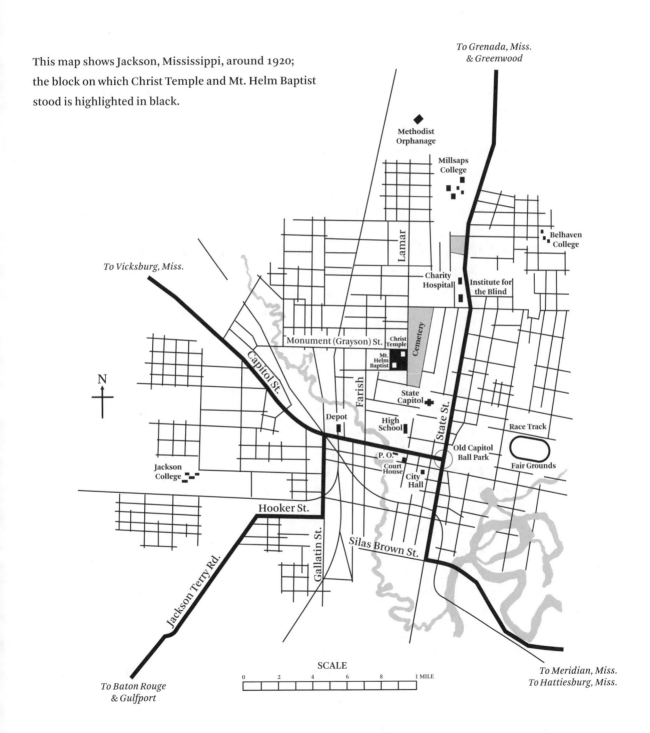

To Grenada, Miss. & Greenwood

Methodist Orphanage

Millsaps College

Lamar

Belhaven College

To Vicksburg, Miss.

Charity Hospital

Institute for the Blind

Cemetery

Monument (Grayson) St.

Christ Temple

Mt. Helm Baptist

N

Capitol St.

Farish

State Capitol

State St.

Depot

High School

Race Track

P. O.

Old Capitol Ball Park

Court House

City Hall

Fair Grounds

Jackson College

Hooker St.

Gallatin St.

Silas Brown St.

Jackson Terry Rd.

SCALE

0   2   4   6   8   1 MILE

To Baton Rouge & Gulfport

To Meridian, Miss.
To Hattiesburg, Miss.

Cautions for Studying Christ Temple's Worship History

These are some of the methodological difficulties about which a reader should be aware when studying the worship of Christ Temple, Jackson, Mississippi.

- Contemporaneous descriptions of worship are frustratingly brief. As with other heart-emphasis approaches to Christian worship, these descriptions tend to speak about personal experiences in and evaluation of worship. They overlook concrete details that would help later readers visualize a whole service. Thus, nuts-and-bolts issues like orders of worship and use of the space are harder to document.

- Although music played an important role in this church's worship and would have been a key part of a worshiper's experience, there is no way to know exactly what it would have been like to experience the sound, feel, and rhythm of these services. The firsthand accounts from the time are short on description of these dimensions.

- Similarly, the published versions of C. P. Jones's sermons might not accurately reflect the manner in which they were delivered. As published, they seem more suited for the eye than for the ear, thus obscuring the dynamism of Jones's preaching.

- Some of the available documentation from the church's first years — for example, depositions of testimony taken during the lawsuit between the contending factions at Mt. Helm Baptist Church — are tinged with hurt feelings and defensiveness. They are neither purely objective nor neutral in their descriptions of and allusions to worship practices.

- It is difficult to find sociological data on early church members or even to identify who they are.

- Because Christ Temple was a church that often used extemporaneous prayer, there isn't much of a paper trail of services from its first years.

- No photographs of the original building for Christ Temple seem to exist. Photographs of the interior of the second building are not comprehensive and date from later in the century.

- Some of the more comprehensive written reflections on worship left by Jones or the fledging church come from a time after the conflict with Pentecostalism. Some come from even later, when the church was stabilizing itself as a denomination. One should be cautious about reading later attitudes and texts back into an earlier period without a contemporaneous witness.

- Some of the accounts from Jones and others present at the beginning actually date from many years after the fact. As with any reminiscing, such recollections are more instructive when there is earlier collaboration.

- As in many movements that see themselves reclaiming renewed forms of Christianity, Holiness and Pentecostal participants often interpreted their origins theologically as part of God's providence. They overlooked socio-economic and other aspects that are helpful for later historians.

- Although there are church members who remember the ministry of C. P. Jones, their advancing age allows them to reflect only on the latter part of his ministry, not on the start of his ministry in Jackson.

- As is often the case with churches started with charismatic leaders, the history of the church is intertwined with the history of its founder. It is easier to find reflections on C. P. Jones than on the congregation which he led in Jackson.

- Jones's ministry had two dimensions: with Christ Temple and with the larger association of Holiness churches he was helping. In his writings it isn't always clear which of the two he is addressing.

- Much of the material available for writing the history of the early years of this congregation comes from Jones. It is tempting to extrapolate from his perspective and draw generalizations about the whole congregation.

- It is tempting, too, to extrapolate from what we know more definitively about other black or Holiness churches — and from the perspective of some of Jones's ministerial allies, especially Charles Mason — to portray the nature of Christ Temple's worship. Some scholars reinforce that temptation by portraying black churches at that time as caught in a sharp conflict between only two camps: those who wanted to rid themselves of "slave religion" and those who wanted to preserve it.

- Readers approaching this church's history across racial or ethnic lines should be careful not to caricature or stereotype black worship and thus make inacurrate assumptions about Christ Temple.

- There has been no systematic, comprehensive archiving of relevant documents pertaining to Jones or to Christ Temple, meaning that what is available can be accessed only haphazardly and sometimes only through privately owned collections.

Significant Themes and Practices to Observe

As you study the following materials, be on the lookout for these significant themes and practices that are categorized by some of the primary elements in worship.

Piety

- The words "Jesus," "only," and "all" in various combinations highlight intense attachment to Jesus Christ as the center of Christian life and worship.
- Christ Temple under the leadership of its pastor, C. P. Jones, was a leading black congregation within the Holiness movement in its region. That commitment meant concern with a "higher life" for Christians characterized by inward transformation and serious, singular discipleship.
- This "Holiness" way of being a Christian led to conflict with early Pentecostalism when the latter included speaking in tongues as a defining characteristic of the higher life in the Holy Spirit. Nonetheless, "Holiness" Christianity at the time was a midway point for the development of Pentecostalism.
- A significant impulse in the beginning congregation was to recover a New Testament name and New Testament practices for itself, escaping its original Baptist identity.
- One of its particularly important practices in the recovery of New Testament Christianity was faith healing. "Holiness" theology about Christ's atonement supported the practice.
- The congregation was a mixture of tensions. It emphasized successful pilgrimage to heaven, yet it was concerned with moral, personal improvement in this world. Similarly, a pull toward ecstasy in worship was moderated by other concerns.
- The congregation would have had moments of being strongly countercultural: its music questioned the propriety of the "world," and it rejected the practices and secret societies (e.g., the Masonic Lodge) of the larger culture. A sense of being persecuted by other Christians and by a racist society would have reinforced such views.

Time

- The week was filled with a variety of worship services. Sundays were packed with multiple services, different not by "style" of worship but by the emphasis (e.g., praise, prayer, or preaching).

- The yearly calendar would have been quite simple, with perhaps only a keeping of Christmas and Easter.

- An annual Holiness conference, presumably including multiple services emphasizing the opportunity to be sanctified, became a regular feature of the yearly calendar.

- Beyond this conference, Pastor C. P. Jones conducted extended series of preaching services lasting several days, often in other locations. This practice was common across evangelicalism.

- Some church members appear to have kept periods of fasting and praying that lasted several days.

- A worship service itself was a communal occasion serving as an "oasis" in the midst of a sometimes harsh existence.

Place

- The names for the congregation and its building (tabernacle, temple) suggested that worship was a chance to come and encounter God dwelling in his habitation.

- Within the church's interior, the areas dedicated to preaching and music were the most prominent, signifying their importance in worship and hinting that these venues were where the congregation most likely expected to encounter God's presence.

- With a purported seating capacity of 2,000, the congregation's second building could have held a sizable percentage of the town's African-American population, which was just over 10,000 in 1910.

- The space's meaning came not only from its interior furnishings and size but also from its location within the city, close to the church from which it had had to withdraw (Mt. Helm Baptist Church) and close to a thriving black business district.

Prayer

- Coming from a Baptist background, the congregation followed a congregational approach to worship planning. There were no denomination-wide worship resources until much later, when the Church of Christ (Holiness) U.S.A. took formal shape.

- Prayer in worship (except for songs) appears to have been extemporaneous.

- C. P. Jones emphasized perseverance in prayer.

- The eventual direction was toward more written prayer texts, starting with ceremonies for weddings and funerals in an early songbook.

- Services could end with an invitation or "calling" for people to come forward to pray to experience God's saving grace or to make a public profession for Christ.

Preaching

- Jones was a dynamic preacher who was often asked to speak in other places.
- The sermons often focused on what God can provide for us through Christ; they were optimistic that grace could be truly experienced by the person who responds in faith to preaching.
- Salvation and benefits of the atonement, whether in initial salvation or in sanctification (a higher life), were a common theme.
- As published, the sermons were logically organized with several points. They had an internal flow that moved from reflection upon God's work in Christ to an offer of this grace and a hope of experiencing it.

Music

- C. P. Jones, the founding pastor, was one of the most prolific Black Gospel composers of all time. Perhaps his most prolific period came in his first decade of ministry in Jackson, despite (or perhaps because of) the tumult in his church.
- Jones produced — and the church used — a variety of musical pieces, including congregational songs, choir anthems, and pieces for smaller ensembles and soloists.
- The utter centrality of devotion to Jesus Christ was the most prominent feature of the songs.
- Jones's music served a variety of purposes. Some pieces were testimonials of Christian experience. Some were pleas or prayers to God to grant some Christian experience. Some were exhortations to other people. In some, God directly addressed humans. This range of music, along with the preaching, provided an opportunity for worshipers to step into the drama of salvation.

People

- C. P. Jones was a part of a collaborative team of Holiness preachers that ministered across the region.
- The fight in Mt. Helm Baptist Church in the late 1890s was among a new generation of black leaders who had come of age in the time after the Civil War. They were struggling to find what it meant to be black and Christian in turbulent social times.

- Lay leaders played an important role in the vitality of the congregations which Jones pastored in Jackson.
- Given the importance of printed materials in the ministry of C. P. Jones, literacy would have characterized the membership in Christ Temple.
- With an estimated weekly attendance of 800 to 1,000, Christ Temple would have drawn a sizable percentage of the black population in Jackson.

PART TWO

EXPLORING THE WORSHIPING COMMUNITY

Describing the Community's Worship: Charles Price Jones and Christ Temple, Early 1900s

Christ Temple was an aspiring black congregation in Jackson, Mississippi, during the era of Jim Crow racism at the end of the nineteenth century. Under the leadership of a young pastor, the congregation struggled to find its way in worship, torn by conflicts within and pressures without. Led by its dynamic, music-writing preacher, the church navigated its way to a new worship home, literally and figuratively, eventually becoming the mother church of a new denomination. Contemporary accounts, sermons, and songs provide the material to tell its story.

Isn't it ironic that Christians fight over how to worship the Prince of Peace? Pastor Charles Price Jones and the people he shepherded in Jackson, Mississippi, knew worship wars firsthand. Jones followed his convictions about the proper way to honor Christ, however challenging. Jones's first years in Jackson were a volatile time marked by two church splits, two lawsuits (both lost by Jones and his fellowship!), and an arson fire which destroyed a sanctuary so new that its paint hardly seemed dry. And yet, a robust spiritual vitality marked his congregation's worship as they fought their battles.

After an 1893 split that resulted in a loss of 210 members, Mt. Helm Baptist Church had

An exterior view of the first building of Mt. Helm Baptist Church (built in 1868, abandoned in 1910), Jones's first pastorate in Jackson.

Source: Lee E. Williams Sr., *Mt. Helm Baptist Church, 1835-1988: The Parade of Pastors, 1864-1988* (Jackson, Miss.: 1988), p. 63.

A purported picture of C. P. Jones as pastor of Mt. Helm Baptist Church, ca. 1898.

Source: Patrick H. Thompson, *The History of Negro Baptists in Mississippi* (Jackson: R. W. Bailey Print Co., 1898), p. 614.

approached Jones to be its pastor. Initially, Jones declined, but in 1895 he accepted the position. One of the most important black Baptist churches in the state, Mt. Helm probably saw in this gifted preacher a reflection of its own aspirations.

To many, this match between preacher and congregation probably seemed providential, since their journeys ran parallel. Jones had been born in late 1865, a few months after the end of the Civil War, to a former slave mother in Georgia. Mt. Helm, too, had been born as a separate congregation just after the war, after having first met in the basement of a white Baptist church in downtown Jackson. Both Mt. Helm Baptist Church and its future pastor became associated with higher education in the 1880s, Mt. Helm hosting Jackson College, an all-black institution (later Jackson State University), and Jones entering a Bible college in Little Rock, Arkansas. And both church and pastor were emerging leaders within African-American Christianity in the post-war South.

Jones's ministry at Mt. Helm started brightly. He arrived with gusto, implementing a rigorous vision of the Christian faith. Jones's immediate interim predecessor, Patrick Thompson, spoke approvingly of what Jones had done:

> At this place, Rev. Jones has taken most rapid strides in the spiritual life and has grown in favor with God and man. It was manifested to him in a marvelous way that the churches of today need the special baptism of the Holy Ghost. God's people need to depend upon Him as their physician, and the churches need to return to apostolic purity. To accomplish this, the Spirit carried him through a special course of preparation and manifested to him that he was a modern iconoclast. He is a foe to all secret societies, lodges, etc., and has induced many of his members and others to sever their connection with them and depend upon Christ and His church for help in the time of need.

Thompson noted appreciatively how Jones had come to Mt. Helm with a "determination of building it up spiritually." He began with a rigorous questioning of its members by "attempting to separate the clean from the unclean" and calling them to a "higher Christian life."[1]

Despite the initial excitement over the coming of Jones, within a few years a war erupted within Mt. Helm between Jones and a determined group of key lay leaders. In this conflict the sanctuary soon become a battleground as those leaders complained about changes that Jones, drawing from a cross-denominational renewal movement called the Holiness movement, had brought to the congregation's worship.[2] When these leaders realized the full implication of what Jones was advocating, including what happened during worship, they saw that his revitalization ran counter to their vision for making Mt. Helm a leading *Baptist* church. What Jones introduced struck his opponents as neither the marks they looked for to validate a congregation's existence as a true "New Testament" church nor the practices the leaders saw in "better-off" white churches, which Jones's opponents might have wanted to emulate.

For example, one of the worship practices which Jones brought in from the Holiness movement was a ministry for physical healing in worship. In later court testimony, his opponents accused Jones of introducing curing by faith, healing by divine power, anointing the eyes of the blind, and pouring oil on the head for healing. Like many Holiness advocates — but contrary to the theology of his opponents — Jones believed that physical healing was one of the benefits of Christ's atoning death. Holiness advocates like Jones saw

After Jones's experience of sanctification and his arrival in Jackson, he began writing songs. Indeed, his first ten years in that city were a time of prolific composition for him. By some estimates, he composed over 1,000 songs, most of them between 1895 and 1905. The following song was composed around the time upheaval began for Jones in Mt. Helm. How might the lyrics reflect Jones's situation at that time?

I'm Happy with Jesus Alone

Verse 1
There's nothing so precious as Jesus to me;
Let earth with its treasures be gone;
I'm rich as can be when my Savior I see;
I'm happy with Jesus alone.

Refrain
I'm happy with Jesus alone,
I'm happy with Jesus alone;
Tho' poor and deserted, thank God, I can say,
I'm happy with Jesus alone.

Verse 5
Should father and mother forsake me below,
My bed upon earth be a stone,
I'll cling to my Savior — He loves me, I know,
I'm happy with Jesus alone.

1. Patrick H. Thompson, *The History of Negro Baptists in Mississippi* (Jackson: Bailey Printing Co., 1898), pp. 614-15, p. 35.
2. The most extensive study of this conflict at Mt. Helm can be found in David Douglas Daniels, "The Cultural Renewal of Slave Religion: Charles Price Jones and the Emergence of the Holiness Movement in Mississippi," Ph.D. diss., Union Theological Seminary, 1992. The discussion which follows is indebted to this dissertation and other helpful communications with Daniels.

Why were Jones's opponents so sensitive about Baptist identity? These lay leaders had adopted Landmarkism. This perspective had swept through many Baptist churches — white and black — in the latter half of the 19th century. Landmarkism claimed that Baptist churches, identified by certain outward marks (the "landmarks" of Proverbs 22:28 and Job 24:2), were the only legitimate churches with succession all the way to the apostolic period. Any omission or variance from this structure disqualified a congregation from being a true church. According to Landmarkism, preaching was valid only when done by a minister ordained by a Baptist congregation. Baptism had to be done by immersion by Baptist ministers who were themselves properly baptized; like preaching, valid baptisms were those done within true congregations. Immersions done by others were not valid baptisms. The Lord's Supper was valid only when done within a local congregation consisting of validly baptized members.

What explains the vehemence of Mt. Helm's Landmarkers? In a tumultuous time after the Civil War, when black churches were faced with becoming public institutions for the first time, Landmarkism's approach, with its emphasis upon rational, scriptural "landmarks," gave a sense of stable confidence to those eager to prove that they were a true church.

African-American Landmarkers were uncomfortable with the practices that had been prominent in the worship of their slave forebears. Worship among slaves was often characterized by a sense of the immediacy of the Holy Spirit and various ecstatic expressions like shouting or dancing, which give a whole different definition to what it means to be worshiping truly. To the Landmarkers, what Jones introduced into Mt. Helm's worship seemed more like this inheritance than what they accepted as marks of a true church.

the Atonement providing for deliverance from the power of sin as well as the consequences of sin, including disease.[3] To his opponents, this idea was too much like the irrational religion of their slave ancestors, not the limited set of marks by which they identified the worship of a true New Testament church.

Jones's opponents protested against other innovations. Some didn't like the optimistic tone of Holiness-inspired preaching; they worried that stressing the extent to which God's Spirit could inwardly transform a person would lead people to believe in "sinless perfection."

Other practices also worried them. Despite the fact that a biblical case for such practices might be made, they railed against Jones for bringing into worship public confession of private sins and the ritual of foot-washing. As the animosity built, some were disquieted by Jones's decisions about the proper age for a baptismal candidate. Patrick Thompson, for instance, who had initially praised Jones, eventually accused him of practicing infant baptism (one of the most detestable practices to classic Baptist sensibilities) because he supported baptizing children who had experienced conversion rather than requiring that baptismal candidates be at least of adolescent age.[4]

Despite how objectionable Mt. Helm's lay leaders found these particulars to be, the last straw was Jones's opposition to Baptist identity and the Baptist name itself.

In 1898, Jones attacked what he saw as excessive denominational loyalty:

---

3. Donald W. Dayton, *Theological Roots of Pentecostalism* (Peabody, Mass.: Hendrickson Publishers, 2000), pp. 115-42.

4. Daniels, "The Cultural Renewal of Slave Religion," p. 42.

Denominationalism is unscriptural. . . .
When a man cares more for the fellowship
of men who are called by a certain name
[i.e., Baptist] than he does for the honor of
Jesus Christ, when they seek to yoke that
certain name on people rather than the
name of Christ. . . . [I desire] returning to
New Testament names and the leadership
of the Spirit of God.[5]

Jones's undercutting of Mt. Helm's Baptist identity had several dimensions which
antagonized some in his congregation. The
first was changing Mt. Helm from a predominant *Baptist* church to a center of the devel-
oping network of Holiness churches served
by Holiness preachers. To support this
network and propagate a Holiness perspective, Jones had started a magazine named
Truth in 1896. And, in 1897, Jones also
launched an annual ecumenical convention at Mt. Helm to promote the Holiness
movement. How this must have infuriated
Jones's opponents, with their dedication to
the Baptist church as the only true church!
The trans-denominational nature of the
Holiness message distressed those commit-
ted to denominational identities.

The issue came to a head when Jones
advocated that the Mt. Helm congregation

In reminiscing about his songwriting, Jones strongly associated one
of his songs, "Jesus Only," with this period. "Jesus Only" became one
of the most important and popular songs that he wrote. It was the
first song in his first two songbooks, both of which went by the same
title as the song. Seen in context, the song reveals Jones's resolve
to persistently seek an exclusive commitment to Jesus Christ in the
midst of terrible infighting. By lifting up the name of Jesus as an
object of devotion, the song was also a polemic against the Baptist
sectarianism which Jones had grown to despise.

Verse 1

Jesus only is my motto,
Jesus only is my song,
Jesus only is my heart-tho't,
Jesus only all day long.

Refrain

None but Jesus, Savior, Captain,
None but Jesus help me sing;
Fill me ever with Thy presence,
Jesus, Jesus, Lord and King.

Verse 2

Jesus only shall command me,
Jesus only guide my way;
Only He to choose my changes,
None but Jesus ev'ry day.

should eliminate the term "Baptist" from its own name. In a series of administrative moves
in 1898 and 1899, a majority of the congregation decided to reject the term, preferring to be
known simply as a church of Christ or as Christ's Tabernacle, which they saw as a more New
Testament way of naming churches. Those who opposed the name change withdrew or found
themselves expelled, depending upon which side was telling the story.

5. C. P. Jones to C. T. Stamps, 20 July 1898, filed as exhibit no. 2 in the C. T. Stamps deposition, Mt. Helm
Baptist Church et al. vs. C. P. Jones et al., Box 13903, Series 6, Case 10041, Mississippi Department of Archives
and History, pp. 56-57.

In addition to internal disputes, Jones's church also had to contend with the external threat of racism. Seeing an inherent inequality between the races was an important feature of this racism. Consider this 1890 quote by another white Mississippian: "If every negro in Mississippi was a graduate of Harvard, and had been elected as class orator . . . he would not be as well fitted to exercise the right of suffrage as the Anglo-Saxon farm laborer . . . whose cross 'X' mark, like the broad arrow of Locksley, means force and intellect, and manhood — *virtus*." This sense of intrinsic racial differences and the innate supremacy of whites was embodied in a series of laws, known as Jim Crow laws, requiring segregation of the races. See Vernon Lane Wharton, *The Negro in Mississippi, 1865-1890* (New York: Harper & Row, 1965), p. 210.

How did Jones respond to such vitriol? He composed somber, poetic appeals to blacks for moral improvement and personal betterment, in the power of the Holy Spirit. In 1902, for example, he published *An Appeal to the Sons of Africa,* which included passages like the following:

Africa's sons

Let each from vanity be gone,

Let each his haughty self give way

And humbly serve his God and day.

Fool-hardy he that speaks of guns,

North, south, east, west, blood to blood runs,

And God who doth the weak defend

Resists the proud, but is the Friend

Of all the lowly and oppressed.

Work! Work! Improve yourselves with zest.

Forbearing and polite, serve well

Your generation: this will tell;

Respect your own, and do your best,

Trust God — and He will do the rest!

Source: *An Appeal to the Sons of Africa* (1902; reprint, Jackson, Miss.: National Publishing Board, Church of Christ [Holiness] U.S.A., 2000), p. 17.

The rupture within Mt. Helm was contentious. There were repeated episodes of personal conflict: a deputy sheriff was needed to mediate rightful possession of the church keys; anti-Jones leaders attempted to hijack a Sunday school meeting from a pro-Jones Sunday school superintendent; business meetings were filled with shouted threats of bloodshed. Perhaps the most dramatic episode came when a leader of the expelled, anti-Jones faction put this faction's new preacher into the pulpit of the Mt. Helm building, which was occupied by the pro-Jones faction, during a Sunday evening service. Jones had to have a police officer arrest the usurping preacher and the anti-Jones leader in order to remove them.

The anti-Jones faction, which was a minority, filed a lawsuit to regain possession of the building, but it lost when a lower court ruled in favor of the pro-Jones majority in October 1900. But the majority's celebration was short-lived. After the anti-Jones faction appealed, the state Supreme Court ruled against Jones, stating that, since the benefactor's original gift had been for the establishment of a Baptist congregation, those who had rejected Baptist identity forfeited the right to the property. An expulsion notice soon followed. Jones's congregation met first in a store, then rented a meeting hall on Farish Street,[6] and finally

6. Today the Farish Street Historical District in Jackson is a 125-acre area northwest of the capitol building

In this undated photograph, Mississippi governor James K. Vardaman speaks to a large group of spectators. At times, his audiences could swell to the thousands.

Source: Mississippi Department of Archives and History

built a new sanctuary around the corner from their old Mt. Helm home in 1903. The new congregation called itself Christ Temple, or sometimes Christ Tabernacle.

Even though the split might have brought some peace within the group attached to Jones, external conflict began to heat up — literally. In 1905, white vigilantes said they had used dogs to track a black man accused of assaulting a white woman. Howling that the fugitive was hiding under Christ Temple, the mob set the two-year-old building on fire. Jones later wrote that no one actually believed a culprit was there.[7]

Contemplating who could endorse such destruction, Jones noted that some white citizens in Jackson expressed their shock at his church's activities, especially publishing, by saying, "The idea of a N —— printing books!"[8] In fact, one of the greatest impacts of the fire was its significant blow to Jones's publication ministry. By his calculation, the church lost

designated to honor the traditional center of black culture in Jackson. The district was the heart of black business, which in Jackson in 1908 included more than 100 enterprises, including two banks, four pharmacies, two realty companies, and a theater. See Neil R. McMillen, *Dark Journey* (Champaign: University of Illinois Press, 1989), p. 9.

7. Mark Sidwell, *Free Indeed: Heroes of Black Christian History* (Greenville, S.C.: Bob Jones University Press, 2001), p. 144. Another account of the fire can be found in *History of Church of Christ (Holiness) U.S.A., 1895-1965*, ed. O. B. Cobbins (New York: Vantage Press, 1966), pp. 128, 416.

8. Cobbins, ed., *History of Church of Christ (Holiness)*, p. 416.

two thousand copies of a newly printed hymnal, a whole issue of his magazine, and another new book near completion.[9]

The burning of the church was a sign of the larger racial antagonism that surrounded African-Americans in the Deep South. The governor, James K. Vardaman, was an icon of African-American racism at the time; indeed, Jones held him personally accountable for sending out the mob which had burned down his church. Given the intensity of Vardaman's racism, it is easy to see why Jones held this belief. Vardaman's racism toward blacks was neither subtle nor genteel; it was aggressive and angry. According to Vardaman, every African-American was a "lazy, lying, lustful animal, which no amount of training can transform into a tolerable citizen." In his opinion, providing solid education for a black man was cruel because it made the African-American unfit for the menial, hard labor forced on him by whites. Vardaman even justified lynching, noting, "If it is necessary, every Negro in the state will be lynched; it will be done to maintain white supremacy."[10] Vardaman was not alone in such sentiments. His violent rhetoric was well-received by adoring white crowds.[11]

Under Jones's leadership, the members of Christ Temple found in their worship an alternative reality to the racism which surrounded them. Despite the obstacles, their hope continued to rise for a better world. A black church's worship was important to this hope — especially the preacher, who served as a prophetic voice.[12] Richard Wright speaks of this enlivening reality of black worship: "Our churches are where we dip our tired bodies in cool springs of hope, where we retain our wholeness and humanity despite the blows of death...."[13]

By 1906, the congregation had erected a new building according to a plan "which the Lord had revealed to Elder Jones" — it was 60 feet wide, 90 feet long, and 30 feet high. With a large choir loft and pipe organ located in the balcony over the pulpit, the building could seat more than 2,000, easily accommodating the 800 to 1,000 people who attended on a typical Sunday. Charles F. Jones (no relation to C. P. Jones) noted that the building when crowded could hold 2,500. He stated that "many times [it] has been filled to overflowing, and hundreds of people have been turned away, unable to gain admission."[14]

9. Jon Michael Spencer, "The Hymnody of Charles Price Jones and the Church of Christ (Holiness) USA," *Black Sacred Music: A Journal of Theomusicology* 4 (1990): 19.

10. Quotations are from the PBS Web site titled "The American Experience: People & Events: James K. Vardaman"; access at http://www.pbs.org/wgbh/amex/flood/peopleevents/p_vardaman.html.

11. See William F. Holmes, *The White Chief: James Kimble Vardaman* (Baton Rouge: Louisiana State University Press, 1970).

12. Melva Wilson Costen, *African American Christian Worship,* 2nd ed. (Nashville: Abingdon Press, 2007), p. 87.

13. Richard Wright, *12 Million Black Voices: A Folk History of the Negro in the United States* (New York: Viking Press, 1941), p. 131.

14. The base cost for the 1906 building was reported to be $16,000, with added costs for interest, a heating plant, and so on, bringing the total cost to $20,000. This cost is not insubstantial and is comparable to that spent by large, white Baptist congregations at that time. For example, Second Baptist Church (a white congregation organized in 1901), building in 1906 to accommodate its own rapid growth, spent approximately $22,000 on its new building. First Baptist Church (a white congregation) had spent approximately $40,000 for a lot and

Typical Sundays, according to the printed schedule appearing in *Truth* magazine, included a sunrise prayer meeting, Sunday school, and worship services in the morning, afternoon, and evening. The Sunday morning service, the congregation's main service, would have consisted mainly of prayers, congregational song, special music that included choral or small ensemble pieces, a sermon, and a concluding invitation. Testimonies could sometimes punctuate this order, as could occasional celebrations of baptism and the Lord's Supper. Other nights of the week offered other opportunities to worship, including prayers for healing every Tuesday night. A few yearly occasions were observed, especially Christmas and Easter, as well as the all-important annual Holiness convention.

More than just a dynamic preacher, Jones was a main contributor to the music that the

The rebuilt Christ Tabernacle in a view taken from the corner of Grayson (now Lamar) and Monument Streets.

Source: I. W. Crawford and P. H. Thompson, *Multum in Parvo,* 2nd ed. (Natchez, Miss.: Consumers Printing Co., 1912), p. 169.

new building in 1894, with Baptists across the state helping to raise almost $17,000 of this amount. See I. W. Crawford and P. H. Thompson, *Multum in Parvo,* 2nd ed. (Natchez, Miss.: Consumers Printing Co., 1912), p. 169, and William D. McCain, *The Story of Jackson: A History of the Capital of Mississippi, 1821-1951,* vol. 1 (Jackson: J. F. Hyer Publishing Co., 1953), pp. 259, 262.

No doubt the larger building for Jones's church was needed for a growing congregation, which would have been fed by the significant growth in the size of Jackson's African-American community between 1890 and 1910: it increased threefold in that 20-year period. In 1890, the town had 3,127 black residents; in 1910, there were 10,544. The actual percentage of blacks in the city's population slipped just a fraction, from 52.8 percent in 1890 to 49.6 percent in 1910. In 1890, nearly 60 percent of Mississippi's entire population was black. (See McMillen, *Dark Journey,* pp. xv, 269.)

congregation sang (or heard, since Jones also wrote choir anthems and small ensemble pieces). Given the number of songs which Jones composed (ultimately, he wrote more than a thousand songs, most of them between 1895 and 1905), it's hard to overestimate the impact that Jones had in shaping this congregation's worship.

Most of Jones's musical work reflects his approach to the Holiness message, including the utterly central role of Jesus Christ. While the centrality of Christ was characteristic of evangelical worship more generally, the particular place of blacks in post-bellum America elevated Christ's importance to them, an emphasis seen in their music: "In gospel music Jesus Christ is Everything — Friend, Protector, and Liberator — because he is portrayed as the Ultimate Alternative to a world that is essentially nothing."[15] Christ Temple's Holiness piety underscored this emphasis even more. Jesus Christ was absolutely essential because he was both the way to and the goal of the sanctifying experiences of the Holy Spirit.

Jones's congregation actively participated in worship. Worship practices retained some of the intensity that had marked the worship of their slave forebears. Worshipers under Jones's leadership demonstrated their deep emotions, some moaning, groaning, and even engaging in occasional shouting while Jones preached.

But Jones didn't allow the worship of Christ Temple to drift too far toward the ecstatic. An inwardly deep love for Christ was what he thought ultimately characterized true worship, not physical demonstration. Not everyone agreed, however. One can hear the tension that Jones likely saw among his followers in worship when he wrote against physical demonstration in 1903:

> Many of us have made the mistake of supposing that to be full of the Holy Ghost, one must be mentally unbalanced, obstreperous, defiant of authority, and generally noisy and self-demonstrative. Not at all. There is no person as sound-minded, gentle, quiet, unostentatious and free from the self-vaunting spirit as the *truly* sanctified Christian. . . . Be not extravagant in testimony or sermon or prayer; do not think the most power is in the most noise. Be sober. Noise is good in its place, but the word says be sober.[16]

Some disagreement notwithstanding, why did Jones and Christ Temple adopt a more moderate approach to worship as compared to some other Holiness churches, perhaps even those in their own network? One possible answer is a rise in social class among church members. Some have suggested that what is generally true of churches has also proved common among

To whom is Jones referring when he speaks of "noisy"? Is he speaking about an opinion that exists within Christ Temple or with other Holiness congregations with which he is familiar? We should not discount the possibility that the more rural Holiness congregation in which he ministered might have been more exuberant than Christ Temple.

15. Jon Michael Spencer, *Protest and Praise: Sacred Music of Black Religion* (Minneapolis: Fortress Press, 1990), pp. 221-22.

16. Charles Price Jones, "Our Weekly Sermon: Abstinence from Evil," *Truth* 8, no. 11 (17 September 1903): 2.

black churches: advancement in social class has tended to moderate the level of intensity in outward expression in worship.[17]

Indeed, as the twentieth century began, Jones — and presumably some members of the Christ Temple congregation — was counted among those rising in African-American society. He was given a very long entry in a 1912 book titled *Multum in Parvo,* written as a "who's who" of Mississippi's "progressive Negros." In fact, Jones was the only Holiness pastor among the forty-four ministers with identified denominations. Most of the book's entries reviewed businessmen and influential women, detailing their occupations, their perspectives on the world, their education, their wealth, and their property taxes (high taxes being a sign of status).

Whatever the reasons, Christ Temple worshiped in a moderately demonstrative way, with appropriate decorum, at least when compared to some other Holiness congregations. Unfortunately, Jones's position about ecstasy in worship would become part of yet another worship conflict in which he was soon engaged. Although this new worship war didn't rip apart Christ Temple, it did fracture the network of Holiness churches that Jones and others had built and caused a rupture in the fellowship he shared with some longtime partners in ministry. The main antagonists in this new war were Jones and Charles Mason, his close, long-term ministry associate, who had been swept up in the emergence of Pentecostalism. The two men eventually disagreed over the proper amount and nature of ecstatic experiences in worship: Jones adopted a more moderate approach, while Mason took a more intense approach.

Pentecostalism had burst upon the scene just as the second building for Jones's Christ Temple was completed in 1906. At that time, William J. Seymour, another black preacher, was leading a revival at the Apostolic Faith Gospel Mission on Azusa Street in Los Angeles, California. While some features of the revival on Azusa Street were familiar to people in the Holiness movement, a new aspect also emerged: linking a dramatic experience of being filled with the Holy Spirit to the evidence of speaking in tongues. This aspect would become the hallmark of the emergence of Pentecostalism.

After the revival began at Azusa Street, multitudes came to witness it, including Charles Mason. With him were two other associates from the Mississippi-area Holiness network, J. A. Jeter and D. J. Young. The men had sharply different experiences during their visit. Mason and Young plunged into the new experience of speaking in tongues and gloried in the exuberance of early Pentecostal worship. Jeter, in contrast, rejected this interpretation of what it meant to be filled with the Spirit. When the men returned to Mississippi, Jones was swept up into the growing antagonism when he sided with Jeter against Mason and Young.

Jones rejected Pentecostalism for several intertwined reasons. Theologically, the focus on tongues seemed to him to draw attention away from Jesus Christ. On scriptural grounds,

Charles Harrison Mason was born on 1866, just outside of Memphis, Tennessee. His parents, former slaves, brought him up in a Baptist church. Baptized as a teenager, Mason was introduced to Holiness doctrine in the early 1890s and was sanctified at that time. In 1895 Mason met and became friends with C. P. Jones. The two, among others, were soon engaged in cooperative ministry among Holiness churches in the region and the annual Holiness conferences at Jones's congregations in Jackson.

17. See, for example, Vattel Elbert Daniel, "Ritual and Stratification in Chicago Negro Churches," *American Sociological Review* 7 (1942): 352-61. See also William E. Montgomery, *Under Their Own Vine and Fig Tree: The African-American Church in the South, 1865-1900* (Baton Rouge: Louisiana State University Press, 1993), pp. 274, 292.

Was the worship at Christ Temple very exuberant, or not? Scholars differ about the ecstatic quality of worship under Jones's leadership. Consider the following.

One scholar describes the worship under Holiness leaders, including Jones, this way: "Worship was unrestrained by normal convention and instead made open to the influence and spontaneity of the Holy Spirit, which, as it seized and shook individuals, frequently excited them to leap, twirl, dance, sing lustily, and clutch at the heavens with outstretched arms in ecstatic displays of devotion and praise. . . . Far from being an embarrassing atavism of slavery, Jones argued, it (ecstatic worship) was a central part of the early Christian church and thus worthy of sustaining. To restrain it unjustly limited the ability of Holiness believers to display the physical and emotional signs — the jumping, clapping, yelling, and fainting — recorded in the Bible as the natural behavior of those experiencing sanctification." (See John M. Giggie, *After Redemption: Jim Crow and the Transformation of African American Religion in the Delta, 1875-1915* [New York: Oxford University Press, 2008], pp. 169, 181.)

Another scholar paints a different portrait: "When it came to consideration of specific works and gifts of the Spirit in the Christian life, Jones taught that one ought to avoid forms of exuberance that could be considered excessive, for they led to placing an unspiritual emphasis upon the gifts rather than the Giver. . . . [Issues of respectability and decorum were] those he raised against forms of worship that encouraged dancing, shouting, or any other behaviors that he considered excessive. . . . Jones consistently argued for dignified worship and an informed faith." (See Dale T. Irvin, "Charles Price Jones: Image of Holiness," in *Portraits of a Generation: Early Pentecostal Leaders* [Fayetteville: University of Arkansas Press, 2002], pp. 47-48.)

How can we explain the difference between such portrayals? Much of it comes down to the method that scholars use to research and the purposes with which they write. If one extrapolates from what is known about other Holiness churches and leaders (the method) and seeks to portray points of continuity between Jones and this broader movement (the purpose), one can draw a picture of Jones leading ecstatic worship. On the other hand, if one focuses on specific statements that Jones made about worship (the method) and wants to highlight Jones's specific contributions within the broader Holiness movement (the purpose), one can see Jones leading worship with more decorum.

Which portrayal is more likely to accurately describe the worship under Jones in Christ Temple? This volume assumes Christ Temple's worship avoided the level of ecstasy often seen in other Holiness churches. In addition to Jones's statement above, here are other reasons why this picture is likely:

- The size and location (both social and geographic) of Mt. Helm Baptist Church and Christ Temple indicate some degree of urban affluence;

- Jones was educated and valued education highly;

- A 1912 book, *Multum in Parvo,* in which Jones was featured included only pastors from churches whose worship tended to be less demonstrative; Holiness ministers were noticeably absent;

- In the sworn testimony from the lawsuit between Mt. Helm factions in the late 1890s, the complaints about Jones's worship innovations at Mt. Helm dealt not with emotional ecstasy but with specific practices (e.g., healing and foot-washing);

- Jones's instructions about producing the best sound in choir and congregational singing, published in 1902, would be surprising if they came from a worship leader who preferred spontaneity and strong emotions;

- Once Pentecostalism emerged after 1906, Jones wrote against exuberant worship services, especially those led by women;

- The eventual trajectory of Jones's church in adopting Methodist liturgical texts and norms in the 1920s suggests sympathy with the more deliberative or ceremonial end of the worship spectrum.

he also rejected speaking in tongues as *the* evidence of receiving the Spirit, as a uniform expectation for all Spirit-baptized Christians. On pastoral and social levels, Jones felt that the exuberance of Pentecostal worship was antithetical to the sobriety he associated with improvement for the African-American community.[18] One's heart could dance in worship, but one's feet should not. Additionally, it is likely that Jones, like many Holiness leaders, was sensitive to charges of excesses in worship, since mainline churches sometimes criticized the Holiness movement for opening the floodgates to unrestrained enthusiasm. (Remember the complaints Jones had received in the Mt. Helm dispute.) Many Holiness leaders feared that Pentecostalism would prove these detractors right.[19] Whatever the reasons, Jones was unwilling to go where Mason had gone in worship.

Consequently, just a few years after the unhappy conclusion of the previous Mt. Helm lawsuit, Jones found himself in the midst of another fight about worship. The churches and

Speaking in tongues refers to making sounds that constitute, or resemble, a language not known to the speaker. Most of the scriptural references come from Acts and 1 Corinthians. The accounts in the book of Acts were especially important to early Pentecostals because of the occasions in which new outpourings of the Holy Spirit in that book were often followed by speaking in tongues.

18. See the summary in Dale T. Irvin, "Charles Price Jones: Image of Holiness," in *Portraits of a Generation: Early Pentecostal Leaders,* ed. James R. Goff Jr. and Grant Wacker (Fayetteville: University of Arkansas Press, 2002), p. 37.
19. Grant Wacker, "Travail of a Broken Family: Radical Evangelical Responses to the Emergence of Pentecostalism in America, 1906-1916," in *Pentecostal Currents in American Protestantism,* ed. Edith L. Blumhofer et al. (Urbana and Chicago: University of Illinois Press, 1999), p. 39.

After Mason prevailed in the lawsuit, his network, under the name "Church of God in Christ," became the movement that grew into the largest African-American Pentecostal denomination in the nation. When Mason died in 1961, it claimed to have 5,500 congregations.

Jones wrote or arranged over 200 pieces in the church's current hymnal, *His Fullness Songs*.

preachers who had associated themselves with the region's Holiness network split; some followed Jones, while others followed Mason. The conflict intensified so much that another lawsuit was filed. The result of the lawsuit was that Mason won control of a large number of the churches associated with their work. He also gained the use of the name "Church of God in Christ," which had been incorporated and used for some of the new congregations in the region's Holiness network.

On a separate path, C. P. Jones became the leader of a nationwide denomination, too: the Church of Christ (Holiness) U.S.A., with Christ Temple as the mother church. The trajectories in worship, which had been launched in the struggles of the 1890s and the 1900s, continued to shape the worship of the fledgling denomination. Jones's compositions became the cornerstone of the denomination's musical life. But, over time, it appears that some of Jones's early, strident rejection of denominationalism, which he had aimed at the Landmarkers at Mt. Helm Baptist Church, was domesticated as his own national church developed. Indeed, in the 1920s, the denomination adopted a bishop-based (i.e., episcopal) form of church government, approved a denominational administrative book, and included in this book written services for a variety of church rituals. Given the form of church government adopted and the social location to which Jones had aspired, these services show the influence of the worship materials of denominations like the African Methodist Episcopal Church.

Despite a desire to follow only Jesus in how they worshiped, seemingly a straightforward task, Jones and his Jackson congregation found the path much more difficult in their first years together. That shouldn't be surprising, because how a church worships is not a simple affair. When worshipers arrive on a Sunday, the pews are crowded not only with people but with some of their deepest religious commitments. What views do they have about God, Jesus Christ, and the Holy Spirit? What do they believe about how God works with people, the use of Scripture, and the nature of the church? These critical theological questions nudge and shape a congregation's worship. In the practice of faith, what is most important to people, and how do they live out those values? Different definitions of what it means to be reverent before God and to be filled with the Holy Spirit, for example, will flavor the worship of a congregation in dramatic ways.

Other factors also keep a congregation's worship from being a simple matter. How a congregation worships is also a statement about its relationship to other churches and to the surrounding culture. Finding a way to worship is an indication of a community's sense of distinctive identity. This statement of identity must take into account a congregation's inheritance in worship: What has it received from previous generations, and what should it preserve from its past? How does it hope to influence the future?

What might it mean for a congregation to be faithful in worship, to follow Jesus only? The story of Charles Price Jones and his congregation in Jackson, Mississippi, shows that the path to this goal is a complex, sometimes difficult one, and when different answers to fundamental questions arise within a worshiping fellowship, it can even be a bitterly conten-tious one. But this story also shows the determination and zeal of worshipers who truly be-lieve and seek to live most fervently in Jesus: "Jesus only shall command me, Jesus only guide my way; only he to choose my changes, none but Jesus ev'ry day" ("Jesus Only," v. 2).

Worship wars have not ceased with the story of Christ Temple and C. P. Jones. The factors which lay behind their initial struggles (theology, piety, identity, culture, and inheritance) continue to play out in congregations under siege today.

Documenting the Community's Worship

PEOPLE AND ARTIFACTS

The Membership of the National
Convention outside Christ Temple
As the mother church of its denomination,
Christ Temple served a larger role beyond
its own congregation. Here, participants in
the National Convention gather at the building's main entrance on a hot August day.
The photograph dates from a period later
than the one considered in this volume.

Source: Anita Bingham Jefferson

C. P. Jones with the Faculty
of the Church's School
Because the church wanted to support and
encourage the development of young people, its members founded a private school
in the early twentieth century. Around 1907,
the school, named Christ's Missionary and
Industrial College, moved to a larger campus about three miles north of downtown
Jackson. In this photo, C. P. Jones (person
#1, seated, first row) poses with the 1910-
1911 faculty. The school operated at the
high school, not collegiate, level.

Source: I. W. Crawford and P. H. Thompson, *Multum in Parvo,* 2nd ed. (Natchez, Miss.: Consumers Printing Co.,
1912), p. 167.

Photographs of C. P. Jones

C. P. Jones appears as a young man in the photograph at left, and an older man in the above photograph.

Sources: The picture at left is from I. W. Crawford and P. H. Thompson, *Multum in Parvo,* 2nd ed. (Natchez, Miss.: Consumers Printing Co., 1912), p. 166. The picture above is from Anita Bingham Jefferson. It's also found in John M. Giggie, *After Redemption: Jim Crow and the Transformation of African American Religion in the Delta, 1875-1915* (New York: Oxford University Press, 2008), p. 171; Giggie attributes the photograph to the Flower Pentecostal Heritage Center.

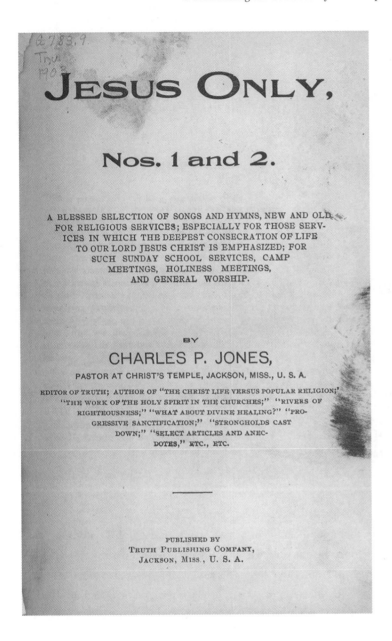

Jesus Only Hymnal Title Page

C. P. Jones was a prolific songwriter and publisher. The title page pictured above was from an important hymn collection published by Jones. The title hints at a central theme in the church's spirituality.

Source: Scan courtesy of Southwestern Baptist Theological Seminary Library

C. P. Jones and His Family outside His Los Angeles Church

In this picture, C. P. Jones, in the center of the front row, is surrounded by his California congregation outside the church he ministered to after leaving Mississippi in 1917. Next to him is his second wife, Pearl, and their three sons. This congregation was also called "Christ Temple." Jones's departure from Mississippi was part of a larger migration of people — black and white — from the state in the late nineteenth and early twentieth centuries.

Source: Anita Bingham Jefferson

Worship Setting and Space

The Interior of Christ Temple

This photo shows the interior of the second Christ Temple (built in 1906) looking from the pews toward the elevated pulpit. It dates from the mid-twentieth century, just before the building was razed. The gallery or balcony extended around all four walls. The pulpit was centrally located and was raised. Before the advance of widespread amplification equipment, this arrangement was often used in Protestant churches to bring more people close to the preacher. Reflecting an evangelical Protestant practice of a century ago, the walls were covered with Bible quotations, including "Holiness unto the Lord," an apt quote for a Holiness church (see Jer. 2:3 or Zech. 14:20-21). The lower platform opened into the baptistery. The door behind the pulpit led to the pastor's study. The choir and the pipe organ were located in the balcony over the pulpit. The church was able to seat about 2,000 people.

Source: "The Spacious Sanctuary of Old Christ" from *History of Church of Christ (Holiness) U.S.A., 1895-1965,* ed. O. B. Cobbins (New York: Vantage Press, 1966), p. 131.

The Interior of Christ Temple with the Congregation Seated

This picture was taken from the balcony just above the pulpit and shows a congregation dressed in their finest Sunday clothing. It looks toward the back wall and the main exit.

Source: "Benediction Time at Christ Temple" from *History of Church of Christ (Holiness) U.S.A.,* ed. O. B. Cobbins (New York: Vantage Press, 1966), p. 130.

A View of the City Cemetery from the Front Door of Christ Temple

Across the street from Christ Temple lies the old city graveyard (now known as the Green-wood Cemetery). Buried in it are average citizens as well as prominent figures like Civil War Confederate officers, Congressmen, judges, and governors. Author Eudora Welty is buried there, too. The state capitol building of Mississippi lies just to the south of the cemetery and could be seen from the church.

Source: Lester Ruth

Descriptions of Worship

A Description of Jones's Ministry at Mt. Helm Baptist Church

The following account was published in 1898 while Jones was still pastor of Mt. Helm Baptist Church. This was prior to the legal troubles and separation from that congregation by those who would make up Christ Temple. The rigorousness of Jones's Holiness message can be sensed in this sympathetic account. The writer, Patrick H. Thompson, served as pastor (from 1894 to 1895) of Mt. Helm immediately before Jones, while also teaching history, English, and mathematics at Jackson College. Despite Thompson's appreciative tone here, he and Jones would end up on opposite sides of the bitter legal dispute which tore the church apart in the late 1890s. Thompson's comment about Price's opposition to "secret societies" is especially poignant, since the second pastor of Mt. Helm (who preceded Thompson), E. B. Topp, was an active Mason and ranking member of the Grand Lodge of Odd Fellows. In 1893, Mt. Helm suffered its first split when Topp led 210 members out to form another Baptist church in Jackson.

Jones was a young man when he came to Mt. Helm. Born in December 1865 and coming to Mt. Helm sometime in 1895, he was likely only 29 years old when he assumed the pastorate of this important church.

Rev. Jones came to this church with the determination of building it up spiritually. He began by attempting to separate the clean from the unclean. In his own language he soon saw his mistake in allowing one unclean member to attempt to discipline the others. It was like the blind leading the blind. After trying other experiments, he came to the conclusion that his only safeguard was to preach the word. Preach!! Preach!! Preach!! Indeed, the result has shown itself: many of the members have entered into a new covenant, and are striving with God's help to be "perfect as He is perfect." The motto of those living the higher Christian life is "Christ all in all". . . . There are still others who have renounced earthly physicians and have put not only the keeping of their souls, by faith, into Christ's care, but their bodies and those of their families. "Blessed are the pure in heart, for they shall see God" (Matthew 5:8). . . .

In February 1895 he accepted a call of the Mt. Helm Church, Jackson, Miss. At this place, Rev. Jones has taken most rapid strides in the spiritual life and has grown in favor with God and man. It was manifested to him in a marvelous way that the churches of today need the special baptism of the Holy Ghost. God's people need to depend upon Him as their physician, and the churches need to return to apostolic purity. To accomplish this, the Spirit carried him [Jones] through a special course of preparation and manifested to him that he was a modern iconoclast. He is a foe to all secret societies, lodges, etc., and has induced many of his members and others to sever their connection with them and depend upon Christ and His church for help in the time of need. The preachers, churches, and people all over this

While this phrase ("baptism of the Holy Ghost") would become one of the hallmarks of Pentecostalism in the next century, Thompson's use of the phrase shows its prior use in the Holiness movement as well as his sympathy for the Holiness convictions of C. P. Jones. Disagreement over the exact biblical meaning of "baptism of the Holy Spirit" would be what separated Jones and his congregation from early Pentecostalism.

country are being awakened by his doctrine propagated by a number of books and pamphlets and a monthly journal published by him.

Source: Patrick H. Thompson, *The History of Negro Baptists in Mississippi* (Jackson, Miss.: Bailey Printing Co., 1898), pp. 35, 614-15.

A Report on Jones's Ministry in His First Years at Christ Temple

A participant at one of the church's Holiness conferences, Charles F. Jones (no relation to Rev. Jones), reported in 1911 on the power of Jones's preaching and musical gifts. Charles Jones was a professor from Alcorn College (now Alcorn State University), which was one of the state's historic black educational institutions. The book from which this excerpt comes is an anthology of socially rising African-Americans in Mississippi at that time. Like many firsthand accounts on Jones and his congregation, this account is sparse in its details.

Pastor Jones is an indefatigable worker. No man is busier than he. Since 1896 he has edited "Truth," a religious weekly, and he is the author of several books, including "Strongholds Cast Down," "Appeal to the Sons of Africa," "What about Divine Healing?" "The Christ Life Is Popular Religion," and many others. He is a sweet singer and a gifted composer. He has brought out three original songbooks, besides contributing largely to many others. The anthems, quartets, and solos which he has composed are many and varied. They are noted for their musical quality and the deep spiritual teaching which they contain. In addition to these labors Pastor Jones does extensive evangelistic work. Besides pastoring three churches, one at Jackson, Pearson, and Terry, he makes long and extended tours. He has held up Christ and helped and won souls in Mississippi, Alabama, Louisiana, Tennessee, Florida, Georgia, North Carolina, Arkansas, Virginia, Missouri, Pennsylvania, Connecticut, Massachusetts, Ohio, and Illinois. . . . Everywhere he has unfailingly and uncompromisingly held up Christ. His message has been "Christ enthroned in the hearts and lives of men."

The present writer is not related to Pastor Jones. What is written in this article is based partly on what the writer knows and partly on what he has been told. The writer has known C. P. Jones for about fifteen years. He heard of him when quite a boy and perchance laughed at the ridicule which was heaped upon him. In 1902, while working in Jackson, he visited the Holiness Convention and heard Pastor Jones preach. He was convinced then that this man was right, and ever afterward the writer wanted the higher experience. The summer of 1905 found the writer again in attendance upon the Convention. On a Sunday in that meeting the Pastor preached from Matthew 23:38-39. Such conviction did that message bring! How horribly guilty did the writer seem before God! That night the sermon was about faith, and he accepted it. Since that time we have been closely associated. Fortunate would it be for the Negro race if it had many more men like Chas. P. Jones. Happy indeed would the race be if it would give earnest heed to the message which he brings.

Source: Charles F. Jones, "Sketch of the Life of Pastor Chas. P. Jones," in *Multum in Parvo,* 2nd ed., ed. I. W. Crawford and P. H. Thompson (Natchez, Miss.: Consumers Printing Co., 1912), p. 170.

Notice the range of musical compositions that Jones composed. This implies that both he and his congregation had some degree of musical sophistication.

This is likely a reference to the kinds of networks of affiliated churches that grew up around Jones or Charles Mason. These networks were the precursors of more formal denominational structures.

"The higher experience" likely refers to the Holiness conception of sanctification.

Matthew 23:38-39 is part of Jesus' rebuke to Jerusalem prior to his crucifixion.

An Account of the Church's Origins

The following is a description of some of C. P. Jones's early ministry in and around Jackson. Sarah J. Thomas-Land, the author, was one of the charter members of Christ Temple and was the first secretary to Jones. Although not an exhaustive account, this description highlights several important aspects of Jones's ministry, and the character of the early church members can be seen: the tension rising in Mt. Helm Baptist Church over a certain emphasis on the Holy Spirit and power, the importance of ascetic disciplines like fasting and praying, and the sense of God's provision despite human and spiritual opposition. The account focuses more on Jones than on the congregation, which is often the case when a dynamic leader is present.

No Congregational church appears on a list of African-American churches in Jackson for 1900. Given its low numbers, the church may have folded.

According to the 1900 census, she was a boarder with Jones.

Thomas-Land is pointing to Jones's experience of sanctification and his successful offer of the same to other ministers. "Baptism with the Holy Ghost" was one of the terms the Holiness movement used for the experience. Later, Pentecostals shifted the emphasis in the term to label the experience by which the coming of the Holy Spirit to a person was evidenced by tongues and other gifts of the Spirit, not the fruit of the Spirit, as Jones likely preached.

I had been in Jackson two years when Elder Jones came to Jackson. Another lady and I were teaching in a Congregational school on Capitol St. Our church was so few in number that our pastor was sent to North Carolina to pastor. Though we were Congregationalists, we often attended the Mt. Helm Baptist Church and enjoyed hearing pastor preach, for he really preached the Gospel. He called us friends, and one day asked me if I could come sometimes after school and on Saturdays and help with his work. He always had so much writing to be done. I began helping him and so became his first secretary and later a member of his church. I lived with Brother and Sister Jones until I was married in the First Temple Church.

He'd held a revival meeting for the church, and everybody wanted to hear him preach. Before he left Selma he'd sought and found a closer walk with God. The Holy Ghost was poured out on some who had glorified Jesus, and they had powers. He attended a convention in Vicksburg, Miss., in 1895, and some of the ministers who heard him gladly received the baptism with the Holy Ghost. In 1896 he put out his first booklet, a treatise on the 12th chapter [of] 1 Cor., titled, "The Work of the Holy Spirit in the Churches." About this time God told him to publish the *Truth.* This same year he was commanded of God to call a Holiness Convention. The Spirit gave him the time, place, date, and even the duration of the meeting to be called. Many miracles were wrought in this meeting. Sins were confessed openly and privately forsaken, tears shed, sinful living given up, crutches thrown away, secret order pins thrown out the church windows, and many souls were added to the church. These were days when the saints were really persecuted for Christ's sake. One time in a meeting at McComb, Miss., while Brother Jones was preaching under a brush arbor, a shot was fired into the congregation. He said, "Let us pray." We all bowed in prayer and afterwards continued the services. We were taken to court after the 1898 Convention and eventually were put out of the church building. The Sunday School Convention was put out at a little church in the rural district near Jackson while we were in session in 1899. We finished our meeting in a nearby church building. One thing — Brother Jones believed in conquering Satan and driving out sin. O how we fasted and prayed! We often fasted three days at a time. Sometimes he fasted so long that he appeared unnatural. In those days of persecution many of those lovely, inspiring, encouraging, and heart-strengthening songs were born in the heart of our pastor. Sometimes when they were given him in the night, he would have us join him through the hours and sing. For he had his own chorus. Often we remained in the church until midnight.

This movement was born in the Mt. Helm Baptist Church. Not only were the members of that church stirred and awakened, but many came from other churches. Some "searched the scriptures to see if those things were true" (Acts 17:11). Of course, when fire breaks out, if not put out, it spreads. Invitations came from near and far, and the minister went everywhere preaching the Gospel — traveled from the Atlantic to the Pacific and from the Gulf of Mexico to the Great Lakes, telling the story of the cross of Christ, who came to seek and to save the lost race of man.

A Mr. Helm (white) had given the church to the colored Baptists. Sometime later these same white people tried to get Brother Jones to accept the presidency of Alcorn College, but he would not give up the leadership of his people. The night the pastor was ordered out of the Mt. Helm church, those of us who believed and accepted the Gospel as it was preached and taught stood up and followed him out. We went into an empty store that belonged to a man — not one of us but a friend. Brother Jones sat on the counter, and we stood before him. That is when and where we held our first meeting. The brethren or trustees rented the Benevolent Hall on Farish Street, and there we held services until we purchased and built on the corner of Grayson (now Lamar) and Monument Streets. I don't know how long we used the Benevolent Hall, but pretty soon all saw the need of a church house — a permanent meeting place.

The lot on the corner of Grayson and Monument Streets, covered with beautiful cedars, must have been for sale. For the pastor and leading brethren bought this place, and on a Sunday in a meeting held here the entire cost was raised in cash and subscriptions. Deacon Henry Moore, in whose home the pastor stayed during his illness of smallpox in the 1900 epidemic, paid the first $100 (as report goes). This was in 1899. Soon the Lord's ambassadors and their co-workers, by earnestly praying and fasting and working, built the First Temple Church, the mother church of the Church of Christ (Holiness) U.S.A.

This structure was a church and **parsonage** — a building that housed also the printing press with its workers and outfit. The Temple and school building were destroyed by fire. The Temple was rebuilt, white friends donating for the work. It seemed all those things were done by magic. The Lord God was with us, and we had a mind to work; and we worked (Neh. 4:6). Not only did we work but we prayed. Prayer should precede always.

We fasted and prayed to know the will of the Lord. When people seek to know and do the Lord's will, He will help them and prosper what they do. Jesus came all the way to earth to do the will of the Father. "Our Father in Heaven, Thy will be done."

Our final ousting was from the parsonage on Church Street soon after we were put out of the Mt. Helm Church Building. Bills signed by "The Committee of One Hundred" were strung in the yard and outside, telling the pastor and his family to vacate the parsonage. Brother Jones was brave. For he loved God, feared and trusted Him, and sought to obey Him.

We were already holding services in the Benevolent Hall on Sundays. That hall was then used as a public school building for Negroes; for at that time Jackson had not one public school building for my people. Now (in 1957) there are in this city about a dozen public school buildings for the education of Negroes. Jackson, Mississippi, has come a long way since 1899.

The half-century that had passed seems to obscure some of the dating in this account. Nonetheless, its basic narrative rings true.

Source: This account is found in *History of Church of Christ (Holiness) U.S.A., 1896-1965*, ed. O. B. Cobbins (New York: Vantage Press, 1966), pp. 17-20.

Testimonies of Healings

An emphasis on healing by faith alone was an important part of the early ministry of C. P. Jones. Testifying to having received healing from God was an important part of the church's piety for many decades. Hearing such testimonies created hope and expectation in those desiring a similar touch from the Lord. The stories also show an aspect of piety that sees personal affliction as part of a larger story of spiritual warfare. Both accounts come from the first decade of the twentieth century.

The second account is from the accounts of healing that C. P. Jones published in his periodical entitled Truth. *Jones's ministry, as well as that of colleagues like Charles Mason, included itinerant preaching and evangelizing. The recipient of healing in the first account speaks of benefiting from that part of Jones's ministry.*

Dumas, Arkansas, 1-19-03. I wish to testify of the Lord's goodness to me. First, I'll say that from boyhood up to 1900, I was subject to the annoying disease called piles, suffering only two or three during the seasons. I spent several dollars trying different remedies, but all in vain. At last the truth was brought to this land, and I readily accepted it. As I'd never belonged to any church at all, it wasn't hard for me to get saved. I'd seen different church members doing so many things I'd not do that I considered they were worse before God than I was according to Matt. 12:45.[20] So on the last day of April, 1900, I accepted Him, praise His name. It seemed like because I'd left Satan, the Lord suffered him to touch me more severely than ever. I suffered continually [in] April, May, June, and part of July. I completely lost my crop, but during all my suffering I resorted to nothing but Jesus. So praise His name — He healed me completely, and I've not been troubled since with that disease. We've a dear little babe, born April 20, 1901. It continued sick from its birth until about June, 1902. The world criticized and abused my wife and me to the lowest because we wouldn't take it to the doctor, but praise His name, we had it on the altar before a Doctor who has never lost a case; so sometime in last June — I do not remember the date — it took with something like diarrhea and continued about 10 or 12 days.

During this period it lost its appetite and couldn't eat anything for 6 or 7 days. When people came to see the baby, they'd try to excite my wife by telling her the baby couldn't live much longer and she'd better take it to the doctor. She'd answer, "We've given it to the Lord, and if it's His will for it to recover, He'll raise it at His time; so we're willing for His will to be done." They kept saying the baby would be in its grave in a few days, but today it is a complete picture of health. They also said it would never walk. Now it is going from place to place by

The testifier is likely referring to a digestive or hemorrhoid problem.

The level of dedication to miraculous healing can be seen in the refusal to seek human medical help.

20. The testifier, Harry Terry, is referring to the teaching of Jesus in which he speaks of the final condition of a person being worse than the original if evil spirits return. Terry's point seems to be about the hypocrisy he saw in some church members.

holding on to chairs, etc. It's improving so fast we keep eyes on it to keep it indoors. Sometime ago, Satan tried to discourage me by saying our baby would never be a well-child.

But my heart would leap for joy when I remembered Psalm 27:14, and to know that Jesus has already said He'll never leave me nor forsake me[21] if I keep His sayings and do them.

Yours in Him,

Harry T. Terry

Source: The first account is found in *History of Church of Christ (Holiness) U.S.A., 1896-1965,* ed. O. B. Cobbins (New York: Vantage Press, 1966), pp. 75-76.

These two testimonies of healing emphasize a spirituality that involves active combat with the devil as part of Christian discipleship.

Previous to three years and a half ago I was an invalid. I had a very serious trouble in my bowels which became chronic; for four years I was unable to do any manual labor; any exertion at all would cause great discharging. My family doctor that waited on me so long pronounced my disease to be consumption of the bowels; the doctor lost hope, so I tried another doctor and he failed; then I tried different kinds of patent medicines, and they failed also.

To report that no human endeavor alone could heal the disease accentuates the power and graciousness of God when he heals. See Mark 5:22-34.

After this it pleased the blessed Lord to send His man-servant, in the person of brother C. P. Jones, to our town to carry on a revival meeting, in which he preached the truth as the Lord gave it from heaven uncompromising. I had heard him once before, and the Lord made me believe he was a man of God. In the four years of my ill health I could not stand night air; loving to hear brother Jones preach, I attended the meetings anyhow, so a few nights that old trouble [returned] again, [and] in 24 hours it had me so weak I could hardly walk; it continued to get worse and worse. The medicine that had kept me alive so long — it failed. I took it in all sorts of doses, [but] I got weaker and weaker. The devil came up and said send for the doctor, then the Lord spoke and said send for the man of God, let him lay hands on you, and pray, and you will be made well.

See James 5:14-15. The language is reminiscent of New Testament ways of speaking. Christian movements which see themselves as bringing revitalization sometimes cast it in terms of reclaiming apostolic power and practices. This sensibility will become a dominant motif of early Pentecostalism.

Praise Him forever. I sent for brother Jones; he came and fell on his knees and put his hand on the afflicted disease. Three years and a half has passed, and it has not troubled me since. Glory to His name forever. After fasting and praying three days and nights for the Lord to be my own family physician, the Lord gave me the gift of healing. So praise His name forever; pray for me, dear saints. My poor heart is set on doing the will of the Lord in everything.

G. Wallace,

Okalona, Miss.

Source: The second account is an untitled testimony found in *Truth* 7, no. 26 (19 March 1903).

21. Psalm 27:14 speaks about being strong, taking heart, and waiting for the Lord. It isn't clear to which Bible verse Terry refers when he speaks of Jesus' steadfastness. See Deuteronomy 31:8, Joshua 1:5, and Hebrews 13:5 as possibilities.

A General Description of African-American Worship of the Period

W. E. B. Du Bois, one of the most highly educated and articulate African-American social com-
mentators of the period, wrote a description of black worship in the South in the early twentieth
century. The account was published contemporaneously with the early establishment of Christ
Temple, although Du Bois did not have that particular congregation in mind. The account may or
may not fit the specifics of Christ Temple. At the time, Du Bois had just begun work at a university
in Atlanta.

It was out in the country, far from home, far from my foster home, on a dark Sunday night.
The road wandered from our rambling log-house up the stony bed of a creek, past wheat and
corn, until we could hear dimly across the fields a rhythmic cadence of song, soft, thrilling,
powerful, that swelled and died sorrowfully in our ears. I was a country schoolteacher then,
fresh from the East, and had never seen a Southern Negro revival. To be sure, we in Berkshire
were not perhaps as stiff and formal as they in Suffolk, of olden time. Yet we were very quiet
and subdued, and I know not what would have happened those clear Sabbath mornings had
someone punctuated the sermon with a wild scream, or interrupted the long prayer with
a loud "Amen!" And so most striking to me, as I approached the village and the little plain
church perched aloft, was the air of intense excitement that possessed that mass of black
folk. A sort of suppressed terror hung in the air and seemed to seize us. [It was] a pythian
madness, a demoniac possession, that lent terrible reality to song and word. The black and
massive form of the preacher swayed and quivered as the words crowded to his lips and flew
at us in singular eloquence. The people moaned and fluttered, and then the gaunt-cheeked
brown woman beside me suddenly leaped straight into the air and shrieked like a lost soul,
while round about came wail and groan and outcry, and a scene of human passion such as I
had never conceived before.

Those who have not thus witnessed the frenzy of a Negro revival in the untouched back-
woods of the South can but dimly realize the religious feeling of the slave. As described, such
scenes appear grotesque and funny, but as seen they are awful. Three things characterized
this religion of the slave: the Preacher, the Music, and the Frenzy. The Preacher is the most
unique personality developed by the Negro on American soil. A leader, a politician, an orator,
a "boss," an intriguer, an idealist, all these he is, and ever, too, the center of a group of men,
now twenty, now a thousand in number. The combination of a certain adroitness with deep-
seated earnestness, of tact with consummate ability, gave him his pre-eminence, and helps
him maintain it. The type, of course, varies according to time and place, from the West Indies
in the sixteenth century to New England in the nineteenth, and from the Mississippi bottoms
to cities like New Orleans or New York.

The Music of Negro religion is that plaintive rhythmic melody, with its touching minor

With this emphasis on frenzy, Du Bois appears to be describing a church toward the ecstatic end of the spectrum used above. His characterization of the "religion of the slave" would still hold true for Christ Temple in that the preacher and the music remained key elements of its worship.

Notice, too, that most of this description intends to depict African-American worship in the South.

cadences, which, despite caricature and defilement, still remains the most original and beautiful expression of human life and longing yet born on American soil. Sprung from the African forests, where its counterpart can still be heard, it was adapted, changed, and intensified by the tragic soul-life of the slave, until, under the stress of law and whip, it became the one true expression of a people's sorrow, despair, and hope.

Finally, the Frenzy or "Shouting," when the Spirit of the Lord passed by, and, seizing the devotee, made him mad with supernatural joy, was the last essential of Negro religion and the one more devoutly believed in than all the rest. It varied in expression from the silent, rapt countenance or the low murmur and moan to the mad abandon of physical fervor [with] the stamping, shrieking, and shouting, the rushing to and fro and wild waving of arms, the weeping and laughing, the vision and the trance. All this is nothing new in the world, but old as religion, as Delphi and Endor. And so firm a hold did it have on the Negro, that many generations firmly believed that without this visible manifestation of the God there could be no true communion with the Invisible.

Du Bois is referring to ancient cities associated with ecstatic religious mysticism. His point is that the liturgical ecstasy of African-American Christianity is a long-standing phenomenon.

These were the characteristics of Negro religious life as developed up to the time of Emancipation. Since under the peculiar circumstances of the black man's environment they were the one expression of his higher life, they are of deep interest to the student of his development, both socially and psychologically. Numerous are the attractive lines of inquiry that here group themselves. What did slavery mean to the African savage? What was his attitude toward the World and Life? What seemed to him good and evil, God and Devil? Whither went his longings and strivings, and wherefore were his heart-burnings and disappointments? Answers to such questions can come only from a study of Negro religion as a development, through its gradual changes from the heathenism of the Gold Coast to the institutional Negro church of Chicago.

Du Bois's idea is a potentially radical one. Rather than seeing the influence of Christianity being (only) from whites to blacks, he suggests that the path of influence goes in the other direction too. Notice his disdain for the "popular" Christian music of the late 19th century. For a similar evaluation of black influence on the start of early American Methodism, see chapter 5 on shouting in Lester Ruth's *Early Methodist Life and Spirituality* (Nashville: Kingswood Books, 2005).

Moreover, the religious growth of millions of men, even though they are slaves, cannot be without potent influence upon their contemporaries. The Methodists and Baptists of America owe much of their condition to the silent but potent influence of their millions of Negro converts. Especially is this noticeable in the South, where theology and religious philosophy are on this account a long way behind the North, and where the religion of the poor whites is a plain copy of Negro thought and methods. The mass of "gospel" hymns which has swept through American churches and well-nigh ruined our sense of song consists largely of debased imitations of Negro melodies made by ears that caught the jingle but not the music, the body but not the soul, of the Jubilee songs. It is thus clear that the study of Negro religion is not only a vital part of the history of the Negro in America, but no uninteresting part of American history.

The Negro church of today is the social center of Negro life in the United States, and the most characteristic expression of African character. Take a typical church in a small Virginian town: it is the "First Baptist" [with] a roomy brick edifice seating five hundred or more persons, tastefully finished in Georgia pine, with a carpet, a small organ, and stained-glass windows.

Underneath is a large assembly room with benches. This building is the central clubhouse of a community of a thousand or more Negroes. Various organizations meet here: the church proper, the Sunday school, two or three insurance societies, women's societies, secret societies, and mass meetings of various kinds. Entertainments, suppers, and lectures are held beside the five or six regular weekly religious services. Considerable sums of money are collected and expended here, employment is found for the idle, strangers are introduced, news is disseminated and charity distributed. At the same time, this social, intellectual, and economic center is a religious center of great power. Depravity, Sin, Redemption, Heaven, Hell, and Damnation are preached twice a Sunday with much fervor, and revivals take place every year after the crops are laid by. And few indeed of the community have the hardihood to withstand conversion. Back of this more formal religion, the Church often stands as a real conserver of morals, a strengthener of family life, and the final authority on what is Good and Right.

Thus one can see in the Negro church today, reproduced in microcosm, all that great world from which the Negro is cut off by color prejudice and social condition. In the great city churches the same tendency is noticeable and in many respects emphasized. A great church like the Bethel of Philadelphia [i.e., Mother Bethel African Methodist Episcopal Church] has over eleven hundred members, an edifice seating fifteen hundred persons and valued at one hundred thousand dollars, an annual budget of five thousand dollars, and a government consisting of a pastor with several assisting local preachers, an executive and legislative board, financial boards and tax collectors; general church meetings for making laws; subdivided groups led by class leaders, a company of militia, and twenty-four auxiliary societies. The activity of a church like this is immense and far-reaching, and the bishops who preside over these organizations throughout the land are among the most powerful Negro rulers in the world.

Such churches are really governments of men, and consequently a little investigation reveals the curious fact that, in the South, at least, practically every American Negro is a church member. Some, to be sure, are not regularly enrolled, and a few do not habitually attend services; but, practically, as prescribed, people must have a social center, and that center for this people is the Negro church. The census of 1890 showed nearly twenty-four-thousand Negro churches in the country, with a total enrolled membership of over two and a half million, or ten actual church members to every twenty-eight persons, and in some Southern states one in every two persons. Besides these there is the large number who, while not enrolled as members, attend and take part in many of the activities of the church. There is an organized Negro church for every sixty black families in the nation, and in some states for every forty families, owning, on an average, a thousand dollars' worth of property each, or nearly twenty-six million dollars in all. . . .

. . . Two characteristic things must be noticed in regard to this church. First, it became almost entirely Baptist and Methodist in faith; secondly, as a social institution it antedated by many decades the monogamic Negro home. From the very circumstances of its

Du Bois describes the broad role that black churches have had in the African-American world, serving as a real center for a broad range of concerns. Black pastors, not surprisingly, often have been some of the most powerful figures among African-Americans, as Du Bois points out. His description seems fitting for Charles Price Jones and both Mt. Helm Baptist Church and Christ Temple.

Of course, the rise of Baptist and Methodist churches also occurred among whites in the 19th century as these two movements, mere upstarts at the margins of American church life in the 18th century, grew into two of the predominant American churches.

Notice Du Bois's emphasis on the affective dimension of church affiliation and its connection to black social standing.

beginning, the church was confined to the plantation, and consisted primarily of a series of disconnected units; although, later on, some freedom of movement was allowed, still this geographical limitation was always important and was one cause of the spread of the decentralized and democratic Baptist faith among the slaves. At the same time, the visible rite of baptism appealed strongly to their mystic temperament. Today the Baptist Church is still largest in membership among Negroes, and has a million and a half communicants. Next in popularity came the churches organized in connection with the white neighboring churches, chiefly Baptist and Methodist, with a few Episcopalian and others. The Methodists still form the second greatest denomination, with nearly a million members. The faith of these two leading denominations was more suited to the slave church from the prominence they gave to religious feeling and fervor. The Negro membership in other denominations has always been small and relatively unimportant, although the Episcopalians and Presbyterians are gaining among the more intelligent classes today, and the Catholic Church is making headway in certain sections. After Emancipation, and still earlier in the North, the Negro churches largely severed such affiliations as they had had with the white churches, either by choice or by compulsion. The Baptist churches became independent, but the Methodists were compelled early to unite for purposes of episcopal government [i.e., bishop-based government]. This gave rise to the great African Methodist [Episcopal] Church, the greatest Negro organization in the world, to the Zion Church [Du Bois likely means the African Methodist Episcopal Church, Zion] and the Colored Methodist [later renamed the Christian Methodist Episcopal Church], and to the black conferences and churches in this and other denominations. . . .

. . . It is difficult to explain clearly the present critical stage of Negro religion. First, we must remember that living as the blacks do, in close contact with a great modern nation, and sharing, although imperfectly, the soul-life of that nation, they must necessarily be affected more or less directly by all the religious and ethical forces that are today moving the United States. These questions and movements are, however, overshadowed and dwarfed by the (to them) all-important question of their civil, political, and economic status. They must perpetually discuss the "Negro Problem," [and] must live, move, and have their being in it, and interpret all else in its light or darkness. With this come, too, peculiar problems of their inner life, of the status of women, the maintenance of home, the training of children, the accumulation of wealth, and the prevention of crime. All this must mean a time of intense ethical ferment, of religious heart-searching and intellectual unrest. From the double life every American Negro must live, as a Negro and as an American, as swept on by the current of the nineteenth while yet struggling in the eddies of the fifteenth century. From this must arise a painful self-consciousness, an almost morbid sense of personality and a moral hesitancy which is fatal to self-confidence. The worlds within and without the Veil of Color are changing, and changing rapidly, but not at the same rate, not in the same way; and this must produce a peculiar wrenching of the soul, a peculiar sense of doubt and bewilderment. Such a double life, with double thoughts, double duties, and double social classes, must give rise to double words and double ideals, and tempt the mind to pretense or to revolt, to hypocrisy or to radicalism.

Source: W. E. B. Du Bois, *The Souls of Black Folk: Essays and Sketches,* 2nd ed. (Chicago: A. C. McClurg & Co., 1903), pp. 189-95, 196-97, 201-2.

Charles Mason's View on the Tensions over Pentecostalism

After visiting the Pentecostal revival in Los Angeles, Charles Mason allowed the newspaper from the Azusa Street Mission to publish some of his Pentecostal experience and doctrine. Charles Price Jones was very upset by Mason's Pentecostalism. This tension ultimately led to a permanent split between these two ministers. Mason's first account was published in the February-March 1907 edition of The Apostolic Faith.

One of the defining characteristics of Pentecostalism has been its "primitivism," i.e., a desire to apply New Testament passages — sometimes the most dramatic or supernatural — directly to church life today. The desire is to return to the life and power of the primitive, apostolic church of the first century. The strand of the Holiness movement that Mason (and Jones) worked in had affirmed healing, but Mason's Pentecostal experience in California left him wanting to apply this primitivism in a more thorough manner.

"These signs shall follow them that believe. In My name shall they cast out devils; they shall speak with new tongues; they shall take up serpents; and if they drink any deadly thing, it shall not hurt them; they shall lay hands on the sick, and they shall recover." Mark 16:17-18

I had a false interpretation in my heart concerning the speaking in tongues. I did not take it literally, as [I] did "They shall lay hands on the sick, and they shall recover." For years God had given me the knowledge of healing, and He had marvelously wrought with me, and many cases of disease had been delivered. I interpreted the speaking in tongues to mean that we left off blaspheming, etc. But when I got to the place where, hungering and thirsting for God, I consented to His Word, I saw that we did not need that interpretation, that the only reason we were not enjoying the speaking in tongues was because we did not accept it. Then I felt I had gone to the end of myself. I had the care of a pastor over many flocks far and near and yet was so hungry and thirsty. The Lord showed me the humility of Jesus. How He came and presented Himself for baptism with the rest. I saw that I should not be above my Master. If he needed the Holy Ghost, I needed it to do the will of God, and Jesus would give me a better consolation to my own heart.

In order to loosen my hands from everything, the Lord showed me how Moses was concerned about Jethro's sheep in the desert. He saw the bush of fire, and God got his attention and got him on the ground where he could speak to him. He showed me how the disciples forsook their nets, and even when they had received their commission, He stopped them to tarry at Jerusalem, that they might receive the promise.[22]

I had a great desire in my heart to come to Los Angeles. I had preached the Pentecost to my people, and they were hungry for it. When I came, it was not strange to me, for the Lord had showed it to me in a vision. I went to the altar, and the Lord put a parable before me: "If you were going to marry, would you be sad?" I said, "No." He then showed me this [experience] was wedlock to Christ. If there was anything imperfect about me, He would make it right and marry me anyway. Then my faith was settled and laid firmly hold on the promise.

As I arose from the altar and took my seat, I fixed my eyes on Jesus, and the Holy Ghost

---

22. Mason refers to biblical stories in Exodus 3, Mark 1, and Luke 24/Acts 1, respectively. In this manner, he interprets his earnest waiting in Los Angeles for a deeper spiritual experience in scriptural terms, with a dual emphasis on abandonment to the revelation of God and patience for God to fulfill God's promise.

took charge of me. I surrendered perfectly to Him and consented to Him. Then I began singing a song in unknown tongues, and it was the sweetest thing to have Him sing that song through me. He had complete charge of me. I let Him have my mouth and everything. After that it seemed I was standing at the cross and heard Him as He groaned, the dying groans of Jesus, and I groaned. It was not my voice but the voice of my Beloved that I heard in me. When He got through with that, He started the singing again in unknown tongues. When the singing stopped I felt that complete death; it was my life going out, but it was a complete death to me. When He had finished this, I let Him hold my hands up, and they rested just as easily up as down. Then He turned on the joy of it. He began to lift me up. I was passive in His hands; I was not going to do a thing. I could hear the people but did not let anything bother me. It came to me: "I charge thee, O daughters of Jerusalem, that ye stir not up nor awake my Beloved until He please." S. S. [Song of Solomon] 8:4. He lifted me to my feet, and then the light of heaven fell upon me and burst into me, filling me. Then God took charge of my tongue, and I went to preaching in tongues. I could not change my tongue. The glory of God filled the temple. The gestures of my hands and movements of my body were His. O it was marvelous, and I thank God for giving it to me in His way. Such an indescribable peace and quietness went all through my flesh and into my very brain and has been there ever since. — C. H. Mason, 609 Stephens Ave., Memphis, Tenn.

Source: *The Apostolic Faith* 1, no. 6 (February-March 1907): 7.

> Mason's description of his Pentecostal experience is interesting in that it emphasizes both Jesus Christ and the Holy Spirit. It's as if he's describing a deeper possession of himself by Christ, and the unknown tongue which he speaks is actually the groaning of Christ through him.

A year later, Mason's letter to his Pentecostal friends in California was published. In it Mason made a passing reference to the conflicts he had experienced since returning from California. He seemed confident of his new commitments. One wonders if his concluding comment about songs was an intentional dig at C. P. Jones.

Dear ones, it is sweet for me to think of you all and your kindness to me while I was with you. My soul is filled with the glory of the Lord. He is giving great victory wherever He sends us in His name, many being baptized with the Holy Ghost and speaking in tongues. Praise the Lord. The fight has been great. I was put out, because I believed that God did baptize me with the Holy Ghost among you all. Well, He did it and it just suits me. Glory in the Lord. Jesus is coming. Take the Bible way; it is right. The Lord is leading me out of all that men have fixed up for their glory. Be strong in Him (Isa. 41:10, 20). The Lord is casting out devils, healing the sick, and singing the sweetest songs. He has sung hundreds of songs. I do not have time to go back over one to practice it, for the next will be new. Praise His name. I sit under His shadow with great delight. His banner over me is love. — C. H. Mason, Lexington, Miss., Nov. 28

Source: *The Apostolic Faith* 1, no. 12 (January 1908): 4.

> For those who have had Pentecostal experiences, one of the defining elements is sometimes the sense of the freshness of a new life in God. The feelings of power, awe, joy, and other dimensions of Christian life are unimaginably intense.

In a later, fuller account, Mason described what he had experienced when he visited the Azusa Street Mission in Los Angeles.

The first day in the meeting I sat to myself, from those that went with me. I saw and heard some things that did not look scriptural to me, but at this I did not stumble. I began to thank God in my heart for all things, for when I heard some speak in tongues I knew I was right, though I did not understand it. Nevertheless, it was sweet to me. I also thank God for Elder Seymore,[23] who came and preached a wonderful sermon. His words were sweet and powerful, and it seems that I hear them now while writing. When he closed his sermon, he said, "All of those that want to be sanctified or baptized with the Holy Ghost, go to the upper room, and all those that want to be healed, go to the prayer room, and those that want to be justified, come to the altar." I said that is the place for me, for it may be that I am not converted, and if not, God knows it and can convert me.

Satan says to me, "If you get converted, will you tell me?" I said yes, for I knew if I was not convinced and God did convert me, it would tell for itself. I stood on my feet while waiting at the altar, fearing someone would bother me, but I said in my mind that if I ever get to that altar and get my back turned on the people, I will see them about getting me away. Just as I attempted to bow down, someone called me and said, "The pastor wants you three brethren in his room." I obeyed and went up. He received us and seemed to be so glad to see us there. He said, "Brethren, the Lord will do great things for us and bless us." He cautioned us not to be running around in the city seeking worldly pleasure, but [to] seek pleasure of the Lord. The word just suited me.

At that time a sister came into the room at the time we were bowing to pray, one that I had a thought about that might not have been right; I had not seen her for a number of years. I arose, took her into a room, and confessed it to her. And we prayed. I arose and returned to the pastor's room and began to pray again, and the enemy got into a minister, a brother, to tempt me. He opened his Bible and said, "Look." I said to him, "Go away. I do not want to be bothered." And he tempted me the third time, but I refused to hear him. I told him that he did not know what he wanted, [but] I knew what I needed. I did not intend to be interfered [with] by anyone, so he give me up and ceased to annoy me further, though he was a man that I loved as myself.

Eld.[ers] J. A. Jeter of Little Rock, Ark., and D. J. Young of Pine Bluff, Ark., we three, went together, boarded together, and prayed for the same blessing. The enemy had put into the ear of Bro.[ther] Jeter to find fault of the work, but God kept me out of it.

That night the Lord spoke to me, that Jesus saw all of this world wrong but did not attempt to set it right until God overshadowed Him with the Holy Ghost. And He said that

---

It is interesting that those with different kinds of spiritual needs were sent to different areas of the building. Mason would have been familiar with all of these categories or labels from his previous Holiness ministry. The difference is that "baptized with the Holy Ghost" would have a different meaning (an emphasis on tongues) in this context than in a Holiness context.

Upon returning home, Jeter would side with C. P. Jones in the coming controversy. These men had all been colleagues in a joint Holiness ministry for about ten years. Notice how Mason describes Jeter's concerns in terms of spiritual warfare rather than as a difference of opinion among Christians. Of course, we don't know what Jeter was saying about the Azusa Street Revival.

---

23. This is a reference to William Seymour, the African-American minister who led the revival at the Azusa Street Mission.

"I was no better than my Lord," and if I wanted Him to baptize me, I would have to let the people's rights and wrongs all alone, and look to Him and not to the people, and He would baptize me. And I said yes to God, for it was Him who I wanted to baptize me and not the people.

Glory! The second night of prayer I saw a vision. I saw myself standing alone and had a dry roll of paper. I had to chew it. When I had gotten it all in my mouth, trying to swallow it, looking up towards the heavens, there appeared a man at my side. I turned my eyes at once; then I awoke, and the interpretation came. God had me swallowing the whole book, and . . . if I did not turn my eyes to anyone but God and Him only, He would baptize me. I said yes to Him, and at once, in the morning when I arose, I could hear a voice in me saying, "I see."

I had joy but was not satisfied. A sister began to tell me about the faults that were among the saints, but stopped as she did not want to hinder me by telling me of them. I sat and looked at her and said, "You all may stand on your heads; God has told me what to do. God is going to baptize me." So I came to the mission and found the brother that I had left, fighting. He had turned the other way, [and] a sister began speaking in tongues and said:

"The voice of the Lord says in my heart that there is something in that for Jesus." And he said if there is anything for Jesus, I want it. So he went and bowed down at her feet for all to pray for him. I was going to take my seat by him. I was left standing on my feet. Then the enemy came to show me what I had missed by being out of the meeting. I would not reason with him, but said, "Go from me." He was trying to get me to condemn myself; when I would reason with him, he tried to show me that it was only deceit in Bro. Jeter, for he knew that I knew his way toward women, but I would not reason with the devil.

I got me a place at the altar and began to thank God. After that, I said, "Lord, if I could only baptize myself I would do so." For I wanted the baptism so bad that I did not know what to do. I said, "Lord, you will have to do the work for me." So I just turned it all over into His hands to do the work for me; a brother came and prayed for me. I did not feel any better or any worse. One sister came and said, "Satan will try to make you feel sad, but that is not the way to receive him — you must be glad and praise the Lord." I told her that I was letting the Lord search my heart, for I did not want to receive new wine in old bottles. But I said, "My heart does not condemn me." Then I quoted the scripture to her which readeth thus: "Beloved, if our hearts condemn us not, then have confidence towards God, and whatsoever we ask, we receive of him." 1 John 3:21-22. Then I realized in my heart that I had confidence in God and did not have to get it, for my heart was free from condemnation.

Then I began to seek for the baptism of the Holy Ghost according to Acts 2:44, which readeth thus: "Then they that gladly received His word were baptized." . . . The enemy was trying to make me believe the way to receive the Holy Ghost was to be sad, but the light of the Word put him out. There came a reason in my mind which said, "Were you sad when you

Mason means the baptism of the Holy Ghost, which was evidenced by speaking in tongues.

were going to marry?" I said, "No, I was glad." It said that this meant wedlock to Christ. Then I saw more in being glad than in being sad.

The enemy said to me, "There may be something wrong with you." Then a voice spoke to me and said, "If there is anything wrong with you, Christ will find it and take it away and will marry you, at any rate, and will not break the vow." More light came, and my heart rejoiced! Some said, "Let us sing." I arose, and the first song that came to me was, "He Brought Me Out of the Miry Clay,/He Set My Foot on the Rock to Stay."[24] The Spirit came upon the saints and upon me! After which I soon sat down, and soon my hands went up and I resolved in my heart not to take them down until the Lord baptized me.

The enemy tried to show me again how much pain it would cause me to endure not knowing how long it would be before the Lord would baptize me. The enemy said that I might not be able to hold out. The Spirit rebuked him and said that the Lord was able to make me stand, and if not, I would be a liar. And the Spirit gave me to know that I was looking to God and not to myself for anything. The sound of a mighty wind was in me, and my soul cried, "Jesus, only, none like you." My soul cried, and soon I began to die. It seemed that I heard the groaning of Christ on the cross dying for me. All of the work in me until I died out of the old man. The sound stopped for a little while. My soul cried, "Oh, God, finish your work in me." Then the sound broke out in me again. Then I felt something raising me out of my seat without any effort of my own. I said, "It may be imagination." Then I looked down to see if it was really so. I saw that I was rising. Then I gave up for the Lord to have His way within me. So there came a wave of glory into me, and all of my being was filled with the glory of the Lord. So when He had gotten me straight on my feet, there came a light which enveloped my entire being above the brightness of the sun. When I opened my mouth to say "Glory," a flame touched my tongue, which ran down in me. My language changed, and no word could I speak in my own tongue. Oh, I was filled with the glory of the Lord. My soul was then satisfied. I rejoiced in Jesus my Savior, whom I love so dearly. And from that day until now there has been an overflowing joy of the glory of the Lord in my heart.

After five weeks I left Los Angeles, Cal., for Memphis, Tenn., my home. The fire had fallen before my arrival. Bro. Glen Cook, of Los Angeles, Cal., was there telling the story, and the Lord was sending the rain. I was full of the power, and, when I reached home, the Spirit had taken full control of me and everything was new to me and to all the saints. The way that he went after things was all new. The way he did change was the same. At the same time I soon found that he could and was teaching me all things and showing the things of the Lord. He taught how and what to sing, and all his songs were new. The third day after he began with me in Memphis, I asked him to give me the interpretation of what was spoken in tongues, for

For Mason, obtaining a Pentecostal experience involved much inward and spiritual turmoil.

24. Mason refers to the refrain of the hymn "He Brought Me Out" (based on Psalm 40), written by the Methodist minister Henry Jeffreys Zelley in 1898. Henry Lake Gilmour actually wrote the music for this hymn as well as the refrain to which Mason refers.

I did not understand the operation of the Spirit. I wanted the church to understand what the Spirit was saying through me, so that they might [be] edified. My prayers were [not?] in vain. The Lord stood me up on the day, and [I] began to speak in tongues and interpret the same. He soon gave me the gift of interpretation, that is, He would interpret sounds, groans, and any kind of spiritual utterance.

Source: This excerpt is from Chapter 7 in *The History and Life Work of Elder C. H. Mason and His Co-Laborers,* compiled by Mary Mason (Memphis: Church of God in Christ, 1924; reprint, 1987), pp. 26-30.

C. P. Jones's View on the Tensions over Pentecostalism

In an undated sermon about various "sects" in the Holiness movement, Charles Price Jones includes an unflattering description of what he calls the "Tongues cult." His critique is pointed and plain: early Pentecostalism's emphasis upon tongues is a sham and unscriptural. Speaking in tongues is the wedge issue that will separate Jones and Mason from cooperative efforts and lead to a break between their churches.

Notwithstanding Jones's disagreement with early Pentecostalism, his history is accurate. Speaking in tongues had erupted in Charles Fox Parham's Bible school in Topeka, beginning January 1, 1901. William Seymour picked up Parham's teaching, which he used in the Azusa Street Mission in Los Angeles (the "colored mission"). It was there that the most public and influential of the early Pentecostal revivals broke out. Jones's terse description belies how vivid and extensive the descriptions of Azusa Street which he heard from Jeter and Mason must have been. The terseness itself seems dismissive.

The Tongues cult started in Kansas a few years ago under a man named Parham. Afterward, in 1906, I believe, it broke out afresh in a colored mission in Los Angeles, California. It became immediately almost a worldwide sensation, and many good and earnest people were deceived by it. It has apparently a gift of tongues; but it has never proved a Pentecost like the second chapter of Acts, and never will, for the simple reason that it is a spiritual fake supported by false interpretations and false applications of scriptures; nor has the supposed gift of tongues proven real. Besides this, many other extravagances, such as false prophecies and indecent orgies, have followed its worship. Yet many of its devotees are preciously sincere and self-denying. Jesus said of all these things, "Forbid them not; for he that is not against us is on our part." Luke 9:50. His judgment act will tell.

Source: Charles Price Jones, "About Holiness Movements," sermon 7 in *The Gift of the Holy Spirit in the Book of Acts,* reprint ed. (Jackson, Miss.: National Publishing Board, Church of Christ [Holiness] U.S.A., 1996), p. 42.

ORDER OF SERVICE AND TEXTS

To emphasize the importance of Charles Price Jones's music in worship at Christ Temple, the following section will begin with several selections highlighting his musical contributions. It is also important to note that most of the longer texts for worship services, which are provided below, come from a period after the one considered in this volume.

One of the Most Popular Church of Christ (Holiness) U.S.A. Songs by C. P. Jones

This song is one of the most important and popular songs written by C. P. Jones. It was the opening hymn in his first two songbooks, which went by the same name. Both the title and the lyrics show how critical Jesus Christ was in the spirituality of this pastor and his church.

A Poem by C. P. Jones Describing His Hunger for Holiness

C. P. Jones lyrically describes the kind of inward dissatisfaction that fueled many people's desire for a second saving experience. He is confident that he has been "converted" but realizes that his life is out of line with what he sees as a biblical vision for Christian discipleship. In this poem he pleads for another touch of the Holy Spirit to accomplish a deeper work of renewal and cleansing. Perceiving this sort of gap between an initial experience and a subsequent one was characteristic of Holiness piety; its roots reach back to the Methodist emphasis on sanctification. The gap will emerge in early Pentecostal thinking, too, although the emphasis there will be upon an infilling of the Holy Spirit evidenced by gifts of the Spirit like tongues.

This poem is based on Luke 24:49, Jesus' post-Resurrection command to the disciples to remain in Jerusalem until they be clothed with power from God. This verse is used in early Pentecostal apologetics, too. Note the different applications: for Jones the power of the coming Spirit is evidenced in a sanctified life "powerful and pure," saved to the "uttermost," whereas for Charles Mason and other Pentecostals the Spirit's power is evidenced by supernatural demonstrations like speaking in tongues.

> *A Change of Lives*
> *(A Plea for Power Divine. Luke 24:49)*
>
> *Lord, of my life I'm tired; do what I will,*
> *I feel somehow that something's lacking still.*
> >   *Deep in my nature something doth abide*
> >   *Which makes me with myself dissatisfied.*
> *I've been converted; this I fully know;*
> *I've felt the sweet fire of the Spirit's flow;*
> >   *I fast and pray, I fear to dwell in sin,*
> >   *And yet I feel dissatisfied within.*
> *My garden is not overgrown with weeds,*
> *Yet 'tis as if some bug voracious feeds*
> >   *Upon the precious plants there growing; Oh,*
> >   *I feel it so. I feel the trouble so!*
> *There seems a mingling of the good and ill,*
> *A constant fight against the holy will*
> >   *Which God hath planted in my breast to reign;*
> >   *A conscious weakness giving constant pain.*
> *I dare not turn, the evil to obey*
> *Yet weakly tread the pure, the righteous way.*

I am the most unworthy of them all

Who at Thy feet in daily worship fall.

A life I have, a new life, I am sure,

But not a life so powerful and pure

As that demanded in Thy word, O Lord.

O yes, I see, whene'er I read Thy word,

I need the power of the Holy Ghost,

Who saves believers to the uttermost.

O satisfy my soul, I pray this hour,

Endue me with the Spirit's grace and power.

Source: I. W. Crawford and P. H. Thompson, *Multum in Parvo,* 2nd ed. (Natchez, Miss.: Consumers Printing Co., 1912), p. 182.

C. P. Jones's Description of the Origins of Some of His Songs

Besides being a dynamic preacher and church leader, C. P. Jones was a prolific songwriter. According to some calculations, Jones composed more than one thousand songs, most of them in the turbulent period from 1895 to 1905, when the turmoil within his original Jackson church, Mt. Helm Baptist, came to a head, and a new congregation, Christ Temple, was planted. The vivid centrality of Christ in Jones's piety can easily be seen in these songs. In the following essay, Jones describes the origins of many of his popular songs and gives snippets of the history of his early ministry. Unfortunately, he gives few details about what it was like to experience these songs in worship. But we can get a glimpse of what it might have been like through the rich lyrics of the songs he discusses here, which are appended at the end of this section.

THE HISTORY OF MY SONGS
BY C. P. JONES

Perhaps the history of the songs themselves would not be understood unless there was something known of the history of the writer. Therefore I shall tell something of the experiences of the life that led up to the writing of these songs.

And what mercy, what grace, that I, less than the least of all saints (Eph. 3:8), should be called upon, after I am seventy years of age, to give the history of my songs! I, who in childhood had a spell of sickness nearly every year, and who was so afflicted as not to hope to reach my thirtieth year.

Happy with Jesus Alone

The Lord gifted me to sing from [the time I was] a child. Among the many drawbacks of my life has been my bashfulness, a natural timidity that has caused me to hide the light of my very faith, let alone the light of any talent I might have.

The first song I wrote and sang was "Jesus Has Made It All Right."[25] Some kind brother heard me sing it at the parsonage when I had finished writing it. During the service, there was a lull. "Sing your song," said the brother. I was bashful about it, but his urging encouraged me, and I sang it. The ice once broken, it was not hard after that to put my song messages over. Praise the Lord!

Then I wrote "Happy with Jesus Alone." This I sang several years before the music was printed. For it was written in 1897, and the music was brought out in 1900.

It celebrated my soul's determination to stick to Jesus and to the Word as it was written

---

25. Many of the songs presented here and elsewhere in this volume can be found in the current denominational hymnal entitled *His Fullness Songs* (1977).

and revealed by the Holy Ghost. Severe trials had beset me. My meetings had been shot into at Lexington. C. H. Mason[26] had started his meeting, but that night the meeting had been turned into my hands, and I had preached. Five people were shot — none seriously hurt. When the meeting got hot and the foe fierce, I had been telegraphed for. This was just following our first holiness convention at Jackson in 1897. I had been scorned by my brethren and the women of our denominational gathering, although I found some staunch supporters among them, such as Elders Richard Morris, Philip Capshaw, W. S. Pleasant, F. S. Sheriff, George Robinson, Dr. R. J. Temple, the father of Doctor Ruth Temple, R. H. Thompson, and many others.

I was looked on as a fanatic by some; by others as weak of brain; by yet others as a sharper trying to distinguish myself by being different; by nearly all as a heretic. The leaders set themselves against me, and those who did not were intimidated by the others.

At McComb City a white bootlegger shot at me five or six times as I was calling people up for prayer. I had preached from Isaiah 32:1-3. Of course his action broke up the meeting that night.

This man had two companions with him, so I was reliably informed. One of these killed him the next night. Then this other went to New Orleans and, in a few weeks, killed himself, so I learned. Anyway, the man shot at me Friday night, and when I (having gone home to preach) got back Monday night to resume my meetings, he was dead and buried. And not a white minister in the city would bury him. They said he "interfered with that colored man's meetings, and had no business to do it."

Mr. R. L. Cotton, a noble white man who attended my meetings, told me about it.

Here at McComb, I stayed with Professor (now Doctor) A. J. Scarborough, one of the finest men God ever made and redeemed. It was at his home that I wrote "Happy with Jesus Alone," which was born out of these experience, and others (Ps. 73). My wife, herself a good, well-reared woman, misunderstood me and had little sympathy with my high spiritual aspirations. This is a song for the determined, the misunderstood, the persecuted, the forsaken witness (Rev. 2:10; Ps. 46). Who can really sing it?

My next popular song was "Deeper, Deeper"; it grew out of my dissatisfaction with my limited ability to do good. The Savior had said, "He that believeth on me the works that I do shall he do also, and greater works than these shall he do because I go to my Father." Not understanding thoroughly the oneness of the Christ body as revealed in 1 Corinthians 12, and Ephesians 4, I did not see how anyone could do greater works than the Savior had done. I felt that nevertheless I was coming short of my highest privileges of service in Christ. I wonder

Here and elsewhere in the account Jones refers to various cities in which he and Charles Mason held preaching services. Their Holiness ministry was never limited to just one city, and they began to build a network of related churches in the region.

26. The C. H. Mason referred to here is Charles Mason, eventual founder of the Pentecostal denomination, Church of God in Christ. In the late 1890s Mason and Jones cooperated to preach the Holiness message across the South. Sometimes these meetings, as in the case of this one in Lexington, Mississippi, about 60 miles north of Jackson, resulted in the formation of new congregations. After the rupture in 1906 over Mason's Pencostalism, these congregations had to decide with which minister (Jones or Mason) they would continue to affiliate.

if I was not right. Nevertheless, I prayed in that song for deeper grace, deeper wisdom, more perfect conformity to and willingness to do God's will. I think, too, that the simplicity and the happy lift of the melody had something to do with its popularity. If ever there was an inspired song, I feel that "Deeper, Deeper" was inspired. Anyway, so I felt when it was written. But I do not say this in spiritual exaltedness or pride. The spirit gave me a song with which to express the need of my soul. And, oh, how many need to sing it with me! DEEPER! DEEPER!

Next to "Deeper, Deeper" came "I Would Not Be Denied." Many have been sanctified under this song — ministers and laymen, and of all races. This song grew out of a distressing soul experience. I was walking in the fervor of constant spiritual comfort. But I was told on an occasion not to give communion. The church was not in a good condition of spiritual unity; God the Spirit knew this. But, as King Saul obeyed the people (1 Sam. 15), I obeyed the deacons rather than the Spirit. My joy departed, my comfort fled, I knew not what to do. I fasted and prayed, yet fears distressed me, and the consolations of the Spirit were denied me, or seemed to be. It was all, however, a besetment of Satan, I know now.

 Having been rebuked, I refused to be comforted. But, oh, how I prayed in every closet, behind every door; wherever I could hide I went to my knees begging for mercy. But no comfort came. You who have been tried in spirit can understand this. Satan tempted me to despair.

I seemed, like King Saul, forsaken of the Lord, who under the new covenant said, "I will never leave thee nor forsake thee" (Heb. 13).

I began to fear the losing of my mind. Satan said I had sinned against the Holy Ghost, and the Lord would never hear me again. I said, "I won't take that. God will have to tell me that from the throne." I prayed on.

Then one night I was given a "song in the night." The room seemed filled with angels, who sang a song I had heard when a child:

> *"Brother dear, never fear, for the Savior is near,*
> *With His hand He will lead you along,*
> *And the way that is dark Christ will graciously clear,*
> *And your mourning shall turn into song."*

And so it happened. Praise the Lord, it came to pass. My mourning became a song. When all the trial was over, thinking of it all one day while alone communing with God and thanking Him for His mercy to me, my soul felt that it must express itself in song; and so was born "I Would Not Be Denied." Out of the depths I had come (Ps. 130). Grace had triumphed. My soul sang unto the Lord a new song.

Jesus Only

Perhaps few songs I have been given the grace to write are sung more among our people than [song] number one in "Jesus Only." Perhaps none has a more glorious history. But it is a long story.

Between the Holiness convention of 1897 and 1898 I began to be impressed with the inconsistencies of our Baptist churches, being myself almost a fanatical Baptist. Our slogan was that we were the only scriptural people, the only people who preached the whole Bible without adding to or taking from — without changing the word of God to add the traditions of men (Mark 7:6-13; Prov. 30:5, 6; Rev. 22:18-19). We boasted of our scripturalness. If it was, "Thus saith the Lord," it was Baptistic; if not, it was the mere tradition of men and unworthy of authority. This was our claim as Baptists.

But I was taken to account before God. "You Baptists are liars," said the Spirit. "You profess to love me, but you do not. You love yourselves, but you do not love MY NAME. You praise yourselves, but you do not praise ME. You glory in yourselves, but you do not GLORY IN MY NAME" (Ps. 105:3).

"It was the NAME OF JESUS for which the apostles suffered shame (Acts 5:41). It was for my name's sake I said you should be hated of all men. You are hated merely for your sect name.

"It was in the NAME OF JESUS that miracles were wrought. You have neglected His name, and you work no miracles (Acts 3:6-16). It is the Name of Jesus alone that has salvation in it. You expect salvation because you are Baptists" (Acts 4:12). (The same could be said of Methodists, Presbyterians, Campbellites, Holiness, or any cult that has degenerated into a self-exalting "ism"). "Christ must be all. Holiness belongs to God. Christ is the life. All else is failure. The Spirit came to show us Christ and the things of Christ. He can glory in or exalt no one else (John 15:12-15).

"You rob Jesus of His glory. You call the church, which is His bride, after His best man, John (the friend of the Bridegroom), rather than after the Bridegroom Himself. Any bridegroom would feel dishonored, insulted, robbed by such treatment. John said, 'He must increase, I must decrease' (John 3:22-36). Jesus gets nothing out of all His sufferings and ministry but a name, and you rob Him of that and go not in His name but in your own name and the name of your crowd (Phil. 2:1-13; Isa. 63:12-14; Ps. 71:16; Deut. 28:10).

"The name of God alone is holy. Jesus is not only the Prince of Life but THE HOLY ONE of Israel. How can you be holy when you glory in every name but His? The Name of the Lord is a strong tower; the righteous runneth into it and is safe. How can you be a saved people when you run into the name of a sect, a crowd, a lodge, a party and not into the name of the Lord?" (Prov. 18:10; Ps. 118).

But I said, "Lord, our denominational name is only a convenience of operation. We stand on principle; on the word; on scripture. We must gather in one name to distinguish us, as we

The desire to approach worship on the basis of clear biblical mandate and example was a long-standing Baptist sensibility reaching back to the tradition's origins in the late 16th century. Jones highlights what he came to see as an inconsistency in the approach: the name "Baptist" itself is not biblical.

"Campbellites" refers to several churches created in America in the 19th century better known as the Restoration Movement. These churches sought to go beyond human-created creeds and return to a restored Bible-only approach to Christianity. Within the movement were the Churches of Christ and the Christian Church (Disciples of Christ).

Jones is pointing out the irony of naming a church after John the Baptist rather than the one to whom John pointed: Jesus Christ.

stand for scriptural principles." Thus I spake because I was a decided Baptist; not that the NAME Baptist was essential. Our history taught us better than that. "Baptist" was merely an epithet applied first in derision to those who practiced immersion to comply with the meaning of the Greek term "baptidzo."

But as I contended, He said, "My people hate My name and so they hate Me. Try them and see" (Jer. 6:27-30). Take the attitude of Paul. Know nothing among them but Christ, and Him crucified (1 Cor. 2), and you will be hated of all men; even Methodists and sinners will hate you. They have all set up their idols in the plains and have the fiery furnace ready for those who know nothing but Jesus. Each wants to set himself above his fellow, but none glory in me. My "all-in-allness" they know not. They do not bless Him who comes in the name of the Lord. (Matt. 23:39, etc.) How can they see Me?

It was this attitude that brought the severest persecution upon me. I was carried to law. Baptists and Methodists held a congress and counsels against me. They reported six hundred preachers present. But I know according to our denominational principles I was a better Baptist than any of them. I held on and was determined to know nothing but Jesus (1 Cor. 2; Phil. 3:1-12).

I admit that in view of the fact that Christ loves all men, and that Paul became all things to all men, it seemed foolish to be so contentious about a name. But this name had salvation in it. It was the only name to which everything bowed. His people had become creed worshipers; they hated their Lord and the authority of His Name. At a bank, it is the name signed on a check that gives it value or worthlessness. The devil knew that was what Christ died for — a name. Therefore they denied His power by neglecting and even denying His name. I had to prove this to them, to myself, to the world. He did not love His people less. Yet said He, "If I be a Father, where is mine honor? If I be a Master, where is my fear?" (Mal. 1:6). "Glory ye in his holy name" (Ps. 105:3; Phil. 2:1-11; Isa. 63:8-14; Rev. 3:8-10).

I had chosen to be hated of all men for His name's sake. I was not carried to law for stealing or murder or rape or slander, but because I would know nothing but Jesus. No name but His. No master but Him. No law but His word. No creed but Jesus. I had to be "happy with Jesus alone." All else was trash to me.

This sounds foolish; but once in a while someone must be a fool for Christ's sake. Does He not take the foolish things to confound the wise? (1 Cor. 1:22-31). Did God speak in vain: "He that glorieth, let him glory in the Lord"? (See Jer. 9:23.) "Thine is the kingdom, the power, and the glory" (Matt. 6). Men have no right to rob Jesus of His glory; that is all He gets out of all He suffered. Vain peacocks standing glorifying themselves and belittling their Redeemer! What could Satan ask for more?

I shall now proceed to tell the story of "Jesus Only," reserving for it the next chapter. This story embraces tragedy. But out of death comes life.

The strength of Jones's conviction rests upon his believing this to be the Lord's opinion. Notice how his account slips into direct speech from Jesus Christ.

All this time I was a young man in my early thirties. But in the eternal verities I was old, for with and in me teaching me was the "Ancient of Days."

Jesus Only

There was a preacher, a member of Mt. Helm Church, named George Wright, who had a brother named William. There was a schoolteacher in Lexington, Mississippi, named Sam Brown. Geo. Wright was a brown-skinned man of medium size. Professor Brown was a large, burly gentleman of decided Ethiopian features and complexion — the type you loved to see. He was intellectual, energetic, brave, ambitious, and therefore religiously "a bull in a china shop."

One mistake he made: in his spiritual ignorance, he undertook to be a champion against the Lord. Both Solomon and Paul declared in the Spirit that there is no wisdom nor counsel nor might against the Lord. There may seem to be for a while, but God lives forever. He inhabits eternity. He waits to be gracious. He can also afford to wait to take vengeance. He is patient, but sure (Judg. 5:23).

There was a Sunday school convention held at Mt. Olive Baptist Church near Jackson in 1899. At this convention I was to be killed. Rev. Mr. Wright himself told the story. He got Professor Brown to come from Lexington — more than seventy miles — to help him. They carried pistols, it was reported, for the express purpose of sending me on to be with my Master while I was young. There was to be a row raised — something the blessed Baptists of that day seemed to regard as the spice of the program. That was a part of their enjoyment. They took it as a part of their liberty in Christ, but they seldom hurt anyone. However, this time murder was planned. One man, a schoolteacher too, a Professor Bracy, drew back to strike me, but I answered him so meekly, and, I dare say, looked so astonished and frightened that he thought better of it. You see, it was that they desired to get me to fight. That would break the power of my message and later the tone of my ministry. No more holiness thunder to disturb flustered consciences! Oh, they would have been delighted to have me fight. They got Elder G. W. D. Gaines with that in Arkansas, and spiked his guns [i.e., got him to fight]. And he had wonderful power before. After that he followed on, but could never be courageously with us in full. He lost his wonderful power to heal and to convince of the need of holiness.

But always someone fought for me. I had armed myself with the mind to suffer, through the mercy of the Most High; and heaven stood by me (1 Peter 4; 2 Tim. 4:16-18).

Directly came dinnertime. Now I seldom ate at such times, lest a full stomach should bring an empty mind and a sluggish spirit (Luke 21:34-36). I generally deferred eating till after the night service.

But a lady whose name I regretfully disremember came and asked me to go home with

Jones's subtle sarcasm reflects the bumps and bruises his soul received in the very contentious dealings he suffered on the way to independence from Mt. Helm Baptist Church.

her to dinner. To my astonishment the Spirit said, "Go." You see, I had to be Spirit-led. Times were too dangerous for such as I to be left to his own inadequate mind, to his own devices.

I went with the lady. She took an astonishingly long time to prepare a rather poor meal. Had I not feared hurting her feelings, I would have gone back without it. She must have known what she was doing. Just before I got back to the meetinghouse, the row occurred. When I got opposite the church house, my friends were all in the road, and the pastor, the Reverend Love, of Crystal Springs, I saw standing in the door, calling everybody back. Brown and Wright, I suppose, were in the house. I do not remember seeing them at that time. I learned the lady's name was Mrs. Fizer.

"Come on, Brother Jones," said my friends; "they drove us out, and we are going down to Carleton Hill and organize another convention." So I kept right on up the road and beat everyone to Carleton Hill. I sat down before the deacons' table and wrote and tuned "Jesus Only Is My Motto." From this song my first two songbooks were named.

Rev. S. F. Sheriff, an exceptionally fine man and a Bible Christian, was pastor at Carleton Hill. With him came J. H. Green, my superintendent and printer and leader of the young people, and Professor N. M. Jones, the secretary of the convention and a number of others, among them A. B. Essex, my friend.

The new convention was organized in the name of Jesus and continued under the leadership of Fathers W. S. Pleasant and Thomas Sanders till the re-organization of our work in 1906.

Elder George Wright died of smallpox in 1900.

Shortly after this meeting, Professor Sam Brown was elected to a professorship in Alcorn College through the influence of a white friend in Holmes County. When he was on his way down, he must needs change cars in Jackson. I was on my way somewhere to preach and came into the station. Professor Brown greeted me with a pitiful cordiality. "Oh, here is Brother Jones. Brother Jones, I want to buy some of your books." (I wrote, printed, and sold books in those days, for I had a limited printing plant.) I sent the professor some of the books I had. Then said he, "Pray for me, Brother Jones. I am not well." He went on to Alcorn and possibly in less than three months was dead. I may be mistaken as to the exact length of time. I think of him with a tender heart. He was so full of life and vigor [that] it seemed a pity that he was cut off. But there is a sin unto death (1 John 5:14-17). Who has read about the millstone (Matt. 18:6; 21:43-44)?

> *"Why should I live, O Lord, if not for Thee?*
> *Why shouldst thou health afford daily to me?*
> *Why should I daily live hopeful and free*
> *If I that life withhold, dear Lord, from Thee?"*

Page 65, "His Fulness."

This is the first line from the song "Jesus Only." The song still holds pride of place as the first hymn in the denomination's current hymnal. Notice how strong Jones's devotional dedication is to Jesus Christ. This focus on Christ is a recurring feature of evangelical worship piety.

This is a reference to an earlier hymnal.

Whenever I hear "None but Jesus," I think of Professor Sam Brown and Rev. George Wright, who set themselves against the Lord — dead now more than thirty-five years. What is their reward (Isa. 30)? They were not willful sinners. They were God's children destroyed for lack of knowledge (Hos. 4; Isa. 9:16).

Men do these things through ignorance and are destroyed for lack of knowledge. Yet often they think they are doing God service. Trouble yourself to read Luke 19 and 1 Corinthians 2, and you will find that Jerusalem, who thought herself especially wise and highly favored, was destroyed for lack of knowledge. O Jerusalem!

Fathers Pleasant and Sanders are dead. Father Sheriff is very old. But their works abide. They were all devout men, the salt of the earth. And they lived long as well as holily. Indeed, they live yet, for all live unto Him, and "being dead they yet speak."

Other Songs

"Where Shall I Be?" was once greatly used, to warn and win souls. A white brother from Texas wrote me about 1905, "Brother Jones, I think you ought to know this. Last night a young lady sang your song, 'Where Shall I Be?', and people began to get blessed and filled and converted and kept it up so that the preacher was unable to preach." This was an old Alabama plantation melody to which I put music and words.

"List to the Sound of the Trumpet" has blessed thousands. A missionary from Jerusalem told me that he had seen two thousand people at once saved, blessed, sanctified, and filled under the power of that song. I have seen it apparently shake a place of assembly with power. It celebrates the Lord's reign on earth. Lo, He comes. It is the hope of the earth.

"Perfected in Thee" [it appears that Jones means his song "Perfect, Perfect"] was born out of a desire that all God's people be one, as Jesus prayed. We are becoming tolerant, but are still saying, I am of Paul, I am of Apollos, and I am of Cephas; and do not know real oneness — oneness on Calvary, oneness in the upper room, oneness in God, oneness in heaven and earth, oneness in Glory (John 17). Have you ever noticed where they dwell together in Unity? There is power, there is life there. Heaven is there. We join with him in prayer in this matter (Ps. 133). We all know the psychological power of oneness in a large congregation and among a determined people. If a threefold cord is not easily broken, how invincible must God's people be when at last they see eye to eye. Then will "God bring again Zion."

"It Is All on Jesus" was written one day when He gave me the grace to pray myself from under a distressing fever.

So was "I Will Make the Darkness Light." I was in Louisiana preaching every night for Pastor L. J. Brunson, now of Bogalusa, Louisiana. I was in the home of Deacon Burton. I had distressing fevers every day, and sleep was taken from me at night. I would go and preach, for the Spirit of truth teaches me to walk by faith rather than by feeling. One day I said, "Well,

Recall that Jones commented near the beginning of this selection about how excited he was to be writing this commentary in his 70s. If Wright died in 1900, as Jones indicates in this text, then this is additional confirmation of a late 1930s or early 1940s composition date.

Lord, I guess that the end has come." That was about twenty-eight years ago. I walked down the road, praying and contemplating the end. When I got back into my room and knelt, as I usually was compelled by the Spirit to do, He said, "Write a song." And there upon my knees I wrote the words, then went to the organ and set them to music. And God has fulfilled every word of it to me. Oh, how many have been helped and blessed by it!

"There's a Happy Time Coming" was written like "List to the Sound of the Trumpet" as I longed and prayed and looked for the coming of the Lord. Who loves His appearing? Is not His coming the hope of His people and the joy of the world?

"Come unto Me" was written in Selma, Alabama, as I was waiting for a lady, whose name I have unfortunately forgotten, to prepare dinner. Some have called that my best song. I do not know, but it always sings well. It ALWAYS sings well and easily. It is a Savior's invitation of love. I've never known a congregation to fail in the attempt to sing it. For always He gives rest to those who come to HIM. And if we cannot come, we can get our friends to bring us. And if we are helpless and friendless, He will come to us.

"In those days" shows that Jones is reminiscing about long-ago times. Notice the cultural developments which have occurred. That a significant amount of time has passed makes the pain he still expresses from the early conflicts over Mt. Helm even more poignant.

In those days without autos or movies or scores of diverting inventions to deaden the soul and steal the time and delude the mind, men thought of eternity and longed like David for the Living God. Yea, they thirsted for Him and found rest in Him. Amen. I wonder if now they are slumbering and sleeping because the Bridegroom is tarrying?

Jesus Will Shelter His Own

In 1905 my church house and printing office were burned down by a mob sent out by Governor Vardaman. A white woman had been found mistreated in a white man's yard in a strictly white part of the city. She said she did not know if her assailant was white or black. But the mob the governor sent out claimed that dogs had tracked the man to our meetinghouse (the one place where we cried out against all forms of sin), which was then a 60x100 [foot] tabernacle. Our tabernacle was built on the side of a "rise" and therefore was on one side about six feet from the ground on pillars. We had built this building in 1903. A strong, substantial building that held twelve hundred people safely; fourteen hundred had been counted going in the doors.

The mob got coal oil and set the meetinghouse on fire; they said the culprit was under it, which, of course, nobody believed at all. It was a piece of malicious vandalism (Eccl. 5:8).

Our printing office with two thousand new [copies of *Jesus Only* I and II] just shipped to me from the Baptist Publishing house at Nashville, and a new book of my own not quite finished, and a new issue of *Truth,* a paper I published [for] more than twenty years, were all burned up, with thousands of dollars of office material, type and presses, etc. The mob would not allow the fire [to be] put out.

But next day friends white and black began to give me money to rebuild — not large sums, for the poor have mostly cared for God's work. I knew, however, that had I been gifted with the power to approach the wealthy, as my friend Dr. J. A. Jeter was, they no doubt would have rebuilt my work for me. For the better whites felt ashamed of this vandalism. For only that class who could say, and did say, "The idea of a N —— printing books!" could do or endorse such a thing. Mr. Vardaman, otherwise a great man, kept that class stirred up against us. Others helped me rebuild. He would not, tho' I went personally to him.

God helped me to rebuild the house — all of brick and capable of holding 800 more people than the one so debasedly and undeservedly burned down. God is like that. He gives our souls great and sore troubles, then increases our greatness and comforts us on every side (Ps. 71).

That house yet stands, and I saw it filled with people last year and years and years before that. Mr. Vardaman and most of his mob met God years ago — a merciful God, I am happy to say. Still I am rejoicing in the exceeding riches of His grace. For, after all, "A man's life consisteth not in the abundance of the things which he possesseth" (Luke 12:15). God bless them all. What a debt we owe the souls of men! The Savior bids us to bless those who curse us and do good to those who hate us and pray for those who despitefully use us and persecute us (Matt. 5:38-43). So this is all on the program. How could we obey that unless we were used despitefully? It is written: "The Lord trieth the righteous." It is sometimes His way. He loves ALL MEN. All souls are His. He dies for all. What if one soul must suffer with Him to save another? In the end it will be glory, glory eternal. And that glory is not far off for such as I. For who has suffered with and for Him as much as He deserves that we should? Surely I have not. Praised be He.

Two weeks before this trial a song was given me as I stayed in the home of Deacon Charley Kendrick of the Terry Church.

I was reading Ecclesiastes, and this prophecy formed itself into words and became a song:

He that observeth the winds shall not sow;
Let them blow; let them blow;
He that's discouraged success cannot know;
Let the bleak winds blow.
    Chorus:
Jesus will shelter His own,
Guide them till life's work is done.
Be not discouraged, the Lord is thy stay,
Jesus will shelter His own.

There were other stanzas, but unfortunately this song, which came out in the "Sweet Selections" songbook and was much sung at one time, does not appear in my latest book; and "Sweet Selections" is out of print.

In 1906 I became dissatisfied with my spiritual condition. I was making a hard fight for

Jeter was one of Jones's closest friends and co-workers since earlier days in Arkansas. He had been a deacon in the Baptist church in Little Rock where Jones had been a student pastor. Jeter accompanied Charles Mason to the Pentecostal revival in Los Angeles but, unlike Mason, would not come under its sway.

This former governor of Mississippi died in 1930.

The destruction of the first church and its rebuilding came immediately prior to Mason's trip to the Pentecostal revival in Los Angeles. It must have been trying times for Mason, Jones, and all associated with their ministries.

righteousness, but needed the renewing of the Holy Ghost to rob my spirit of that hardness that makes a man a "pulpit scold" rather than a shepherd who gives his life for the sheep in tender love.

The Lord sent along at this time a man (with his wife) from Chicago named Brother Norton. He heard me preach and perceived that I needed another anointing with a fuller view of the atonement, the all-sufficiency of Christ and His blood and His finished work and HIS COMPLETE SALVATION. He perceived that I had become a scolder. Through his visits I was set seeking a renewing of the Holy Ghost (Titus 3:5). I gave myself to three or four days of fasting for this. At last I got a new vision of Jesus and His all-in-allness; the power of His atonement, the all-sufficiency of HIS Holy merits; a new view of the cross and what it meant. Oh, the rest and victory of faith! For the Holy Ghost does not speak of Himself but takes the things of Christ and shows them to us. After law, the gospel. The mind of Christ. Bread instead of stones. Christ the One Life gives us in resurrection glory.

Out of this glorious renewing was born the songs "Jesus Christ Is Made to Me All I Need" and "O Hide Me" and several other songs that were much used by the Holy Spirit to save and comfort souls. Amen.

I have written more than a thousand songs, most of them born out of significant experiences — experiences of trial or of victory or both. Of this class is "I Will Not Yield," which was written in New Haven, Conn., in 1906. This song was greatly used by J. T. Brown, the evangelist, formerly of Nashville, Tenn., now of San Diego, California.

Also, "I'll Go All the Way with My Savior," written in Americus, Georgia, in the home of Professor A. S. Staley. [It cannot be determined to which song Jones is referring.] "Happy Day at Hand" was written in the home of Deacon Geo. O. Freeman, one of the truly great businessmen who was with us. I was on my way to Lexington, Mississippi, to a convention. I was in my room at prayer, for in those days of strenuous seeking after God and souls we literally "gave ourselves to the word of God and prayer." And what a wonderful occupation for the young! It bears rich fruit and gives sweet memories in after years.

As I knelt and wrote, the vision unfolded to my soul. And when I got to Lexington, the song took the convention. At Jackson an amusing thing was said. They had a way of mocking me about praising the Lord. Men at work would mock me as I went along the street, calling the attention of one another to my nearness by saying, "Praise the Lord." This never hurt me or aroused resentment in me. I knew they were spiritually ignorant. So I would say to myself, "Thank God, I've got you praising Him somehow"; as Paul said to the Philippians, *"So Christ is preached"* (Phil. 1). When I sang this "Happy Day at Hand" in Jackson, they said, "You can't do anything with Brother Jones now; he's got him a song, 'Praise the Lord.' " And so grace conquered.

"O How Sad to Have Lived" or "The Harvest Is Past," so greatly used in the ministry of Bishop Jeter, was written in the home of a merchant in Okolona, Mississippi. His name was Mr. McIntosh. His was my first home in that city.

Here as elsewhere, Jones uses fragments and inverted words for poetic emphasis.

The extent of Jones's ministry and the breadth of his travels can be seen in the cities which he lists.

One song that was greatly used in my ministry is "The Strong Man Bound." This was the result of a revelation of the truth that Christ had already conquered for us and that we are more than conquerors by our experiences, "through Him that loved us and gave Himself for us" (Rom. 8:26-39). Truly Jesus is mighty to save.

Two other songs, "There's Coming a Time," so greatly used by Geo. H. Thomas, and "Precious Savior," have a great history of service. Souls break down under them. But they were simply born out of deep conviction and intense longing after God and the salvation of men.

All of my greatest songs were written before I was fifty years of age, most of them before I was forty.

Jones turned 40 in December 1905 and 50 in 1915.

Truly it is good for a man to bear the yoke in his youth (Lam. 3). David's and Solomon's and Paul's greatest work was done when they were young men. So were Isaiah's, Jeremiah's, and Ezekiel's. And M. Spurgeon's. Do not wait for old age to serve God. Remember thy Creator in the days of thy youth. Give unto the Lord glory and strength (Ps. 28; Ps. 96 and 94). The king hath desired thy beauty — the beauty of youth.

Source: "The History of My Songs" by C. P. Jones can be found in *History of Church of Christ (Holiness) U.S.A.,* ed. O. B. Cobbins (New York: Vantage Press, 1966), pp. 400-419. Along with Jones's autobiographical sketch, it has been reprinted in *The Journal of Black Sacred Music* 2 (Fall 1988): 60-80.

Here are the lyrics to the songs Jones mentioned in his history. Typically, the refrain is repeated after each verse.

Jesus Has Made It All Right

Verse 1

I once was a self-banished soul from the Lord,
And wandered to death in my flight,
Till Jesus o'ertook me, all sin-sick and sore,
And ventured to make it all right.

Refrain

All right, all right; Jesus has made it all right;
The Father accepts me, Salvation is sure;
For Jesus has made it all right.

Verse 2

It cost Him a life of abasement so sad,
And many a pray'r-laden night;
It cost Him a death of great anguish and pain:
But now He has made it all right.

Verse 3

He rose from the grave all triumphant o'er sin,
Ascending to heaven in might;
There at the right hand of the Father to plead.
Come, sinner, He'll make it all right.

Verse 4

Say not, "I am too mean a sinner to come,"
And give up the struggle tonight;
Arise, for the Savior is calling for thee;
Come, Jesus will make it all right.

Deeper, Deeper

Verse 1

Deeper, deeper in the love of Jesus

Daily let me go;

Higher, higher in the school of wisdom,

More of grace to know.

Refrain

O deeper yet, I pray,

And higher ev'ry day,

And wiser, blessed Lord,

In thy precious, holy word.

Verse 2

Deeper, deeper! Blessed Holy Spirit,

Take me deeper still,

Till my life is wholly lost in Jesus

And His perfect will.

Verse 3

Deeper, deeper! Tho' it cost hard trials,

Deeper let me go!

Rooted in the holy love of Jesus,

Let me fruitful grow.

Verse 4

Deeper, higher ev'ry day in Jesus,

Till all conflict past

Finds me conquer'r, and in His own image

Perfected at last

Verse 5

Deeper, deeper in the faith of Jesus,

Holy faith and true:

In His pow'r and soul exalting wisdom

Let me peace pursue.

I Would Not Be Denied

Verse 1

When pangs of death seized on my soul,

Unto the Lord I cried;

Till Jesus came and made me whole,

I would not be denied.

Refrain

I would not be denied, I would not be denied,

Till Jesus came and made me whole, I would not be denied.

Verse 2

As Jacob in the days of old,

I wrestled with the Lord;

And instant, with a courage bold,

I stood upon His Word.

Verse 3

Old Satan said my Lord was gone

And would not hear my prayer;

But praise the Lord, the work is done,

And Christ the Lord is here.

Where Shall I Be?

Verse 1

When judgment day is drawing nigh, Where shall I be?

When God the works of men shall try, Where shall I be?

When east and west the fire shall roll, Where shall I be?

How will it be with my poor soul; Where shall I be?

Refrain

O where shall I be when the first trumpet sounds,

O where shall I be when it sounds so loud?

When it sounds so loud as to wake up the dead?

O where shall I be when it sounds?

Verse 2

When wicked men His wrath shall see, Where shall I be?

And to the rocks and mountains flee, Where shall I be?

When hills and mountains flee away, Where shall I be?

When all the works of men decay, Where shall I be?

Verse 3

When heav'n and earth as some great scroll, Where shall I be?

Shall from God's angry presence roll, Where shall I be?

When all the saints redeemed shall stand, Where shall I be?

Forever blest at God's right hand, Where shall I be?

Verse 4

All trouble done, all conflict past, Where shall I be?

And old Apolyon bound at last, Where shall I be?

When Christ shall reign from shore to shore, Where shall I be?

And peace abide forevermore, Where shall I be?

List to the Sound of the Trumpet

(also known as "The March of Zion's King")

Verse 1

List to the sound of the trumpet, 'tis the coming of the King!

List how the saints are shouting, and the very heavens ring.

Lift up your heads, ye pilgrims, there's a message from the sky;

'Tis the hour of your redemption, and the King is nigh.

Refrain

Lo, He comes! (Hear the glad cry!) Lo, He comes!

    (Lo, He comes!)

Lo, He comes! (Behold Him nigh!) Coming to earth again!

Lo, He comes! (Hear the glad cry!) Lo, He comes!

    (Lo, He comes!)

Shout, ye ransomed! Hail the coming of the King! (of the King!)

Verse 2

O what a weeping and wailing, from among the sinful throng!

They have no part forever in the saints' redemption song.

It is their hour of judgment, and the judge of earth and sky,

Cloth'd in the robes of vengeance, draweth nigh, yes, nigh.

Verse 3

List to the sound of the trumpet, 'tis the year of jubilee!

And this old earth from oppression shall a thousand years

    be free;

It is the march of the Savior, come the church's tears to dry,

'Tis the hallelujah morning, for the King is nigh.

It Is All on Jesus (also known as "All on Jesus")

Verse 1

It is all on Jesus, yes indeed,

I've laid it there this hour;

My ev'ry pain and care and need,

I am resting in His power.

Refrain

Yes, it's all on Jesus, ev'ry whit on Jesus,

All on Jesus, and I am free;

He bore my sins and sickness in His body

On the shameful cross of Calvary.

Verse 2

It is all on Jesus, bless the Lord!

The load I no more carry;

I am trusting in His holy word;

My heart is joyful, very!

Verse 3

It is all on Jesus; yes, by faith

I've laid on Him my sorrow;

I have no trouble, have no wrath,

And none expect to borrow.

Verse 4

It is all on Jesus, O how free!

O what a wondrous Savior

To give His precious life for me,

And show to me such favor!

I Will Make the Darkness Light

Verse 1

I will make the darkness light before thee,

What is wrong I'll make it right before thee,

All thy battles I will fight before thee,

And the high place I'll bring down.

Refrain

When thou walkest by the way I'll lead thee,

On the fatness of the land I'll feed thee,

And a mansion in the sky I'll deed thee,

And the high place I'll bring down.

Verse 2

With an everlasting love I'll love thee,

Tho' with trials deep and sore I'll prove thee,

But there's nothing that can hurt or move thee,

And the high place I'll bring down.

Verse 3

Although Satan in his rage would tear thee,

And with all his winning arts would snare thee,

Even down to thine old age I'll bear thee,

And the high place I'll bring down.

Verse 4

I will make the darkness light before thee,

I will make the crooked straight before thee,

I will spread my wings protecting o'er thee,

And the high place I'll bring down.

There's a Happy Time Coming

(also known as "There's a Happy Time A-coming")

Verse 1

There's a happy time a-coming, there's a happy time a-coming,

When oppressors shall no longer sit on high,

When the proud shall be as stubble,

      for their sins receiving double;

There's a happy time a-coming by and by.

Refrain

Let us wait (Let us wait) and labor on (and labor on),

Soon the vict'ry (Soon the vict'ry) will be won (will be won),

Soon our suff'ring (Soon our suff'ring) will be done

      (will be done)

— There's a happy time a-coming by and by.

Verse 2

Lo, the Lord will come from heaven on the clouds

      with thunder riven,

And the angel host will follow in His train;

He'll redeem the world from sadness, and His servants fill

      with gladness

When in power He shall come to earth again.

Verse 3

Let us wait and labor, brother, loving, helping one another,

Walking meekly in the laws of God most high;

Let us bear reproach and sorrow, 'twill be better on tomorrow

— There's a happy day a-coming by and by.

Come unto Me

Verse 1

Hear the blessed Savior calling the oppressed,

"Oh, ye heavy-laden, come to Me and rest;

Come, no longer tarry, I your load will bear,

Bring Me every burden, bring Me every care."

Refrain

Come unto Me, I will give you rest;

Take My yoke upon you, hear Me and be blest;

I am meek and lowly, come and trust My might;

Come, My yoke is easy, and My burden's light.

Verse 2

Are you disappointed, wand'ring here and there,

Dragging chains of doubt and loaded down with care?

Do unholy feelings struggle in your breast?

Bring your case to Jesus — He will give you rest.

Verse 3

Stumbling on the mountains dark with sin and shame,

Stumbling toward the pit of hell's consuming flame;

By the pow'rs of sin deluded and oppressed,

Hear the tender Shepherd, "Come to Me and rest."

Verse 4

Have you cares of business, cares of pressing debt?

Cares of social life or cares of hope unmet?

Are you by remorse or sense of guilt depressed?

Come right on to Jesus, He will give you rest.

Verse 5

Have you by temptation often conquered been,

Has a sense of weakness brought distress within?

Christ will sanctify you, if you'll claim His best;

In the Holy Spirit, he will give you rest.

All I Need

Verse 1

Jesus Christ is made to me,

All I need, all I need,

He alone, is all my plea,

He is all I need.

Refrain

Wisdom, righteousness, and pow'r,

Holiness forevermore,

My redemption full and sure,

He is all I need.

Verse 2

Jesus is my all in all,

All I need, all I need,

While He keeps I cannot fall,

He is all I need.

Verse 3

He redeemed me when He died,

All I need, all I need,

I with Him was crucified,

He is all I need.

Verse 4

To My Savior will I cleave,

All I need, all I need,

He will not His servant leave,

He is all I need.

Verse 5

He's the treasure of my soul,

All I need, all I need,

He hath cleansed and made me whole,

He is all I need.

Verse 6

Glory, glory to the Lamb,

All I need, all I need,

By His spirit sealed I am,

He is all I need.

O Hide Me

Verse 1

My soul, O Lord, is much distressed,

I flee unto Thee to hide me;

Where else, O Lord, can a soul find rest?

I flee unto Thee to hide me.

Refrain

O hide me from the hidden foe,

O hide me from a world of woe,

O keep my feet where-'er I go,

I flee unto Thee to hide me.

Verse 2

When storms arise and thunders roar,

I flee unto Thee to hide me;

Though I am weak, despised and poor,

I flee unto Thee to hide me.

Verse 3

From strong temptation, blessed Lord,

I flee unto Thee to hide me;

O keep me by Thy holy Word,

I flee unto Thee to hide me.

Verse 4

When demons seek to fill with dread,

I flee unto Thee to hide me;

When sickness binds me to my bed,

I flee unto Thee to hide me.

Verse 5

When evil men my soul would slay,

I flee unto Thee to hide me;

From ev'ry danger on life's way,

I flee unto Thee to hide me.

Verse 6

Until our Lord shall come again,

I flee unto Thee to hide me;

Till everlasting peace shall reign,

I flee unto Thee to hide me.

I Will Not Yield

Verse 1

I will not yield to the tempter,
I will not yield to sin,
God's power is able to keep me,
I will the vict'ry win.

Refrain

I will not yield, I will be free,
Sin shall no more reign over me,
God will sufficient grace supply,
Before I'll yield, I'll die!

Verse 2

I will not yield to the tempter,
Christ died to set me free,
And rose for my justification,
And I will perfect be.

Verse 3

I will not yield to the tempter,
All heav'n to help me stands,
God plenteous grace will supply me,
Nor leave me in his hands.

Verse 4

I will not yield to the tempter,
God doth my heart incline
To yield myself to the Spirit
And do His will divine.

Verse 5

I will not yield to the tempter,
Let who will, walk in sin;
For he who today overcometh,
A crown of life shall win.

Verse 6

I will not yield to the tempter,
My soul is glory bound;
When Jesus cometh to claim me,
I would be spotless found.

Happy Day at Hand

(also known as "There's a Happy Day at Hand")

Verse 1

There's a happy day at hand, Hallelujah!

We have struck the Holy Land, Praise the Lord!

We have cross'd the muddy tide, Hallelujah!

We are now on Canaan's side, Praise the Lord!

Refrain

Tho' the conquest lies ahead, we shall conquer,
          never dread,

All the land our feet shall tread, Praise the Lord!

Tho' the conquest lies ahead, we shall conquer,
          never dread,

All the land our feet shall tread, Praise the Lord!

Verse 2

'Tis the milk and honey land, Hallelujah!

We by faith upon it stand, Praise the Lord!

It is rich in all we need, Hallelujah!

Living water, living bread, Praise the Lord!

Verse 3

There the cities great and high, Hallelujah!

Strong and wall'd up t'ward the sky, Praise the Lord!

But by faith we'll bring them low, Hallelujah!

And Jehovah's pow'r we'll show, Praise the Lord!

Verse 4

There are giants tall and grand, Hallelujah!

Stalking proudly thro' this land, Praise the Lord!

But we'll trust the name of God, Hallelujah!

And we'll bring them to the sod, Praise the Lord!

Verse 5

Never let your spirits fall, Hallelujah!

Only let the Lord be all, Praise the Lord!

By the Spirit He doth give, Hallelujah!

We shall conquer while we live, Praise the Lord!

Verse 6

Tho' at Ai come defeat, Hallelujah!

And reproach upon us beat, Praise the Lord!

We will search the camp for sin, Hallelujah!

And renew the fight again, Praise the Lord!

Verse 7

Blessed land of holiness, Hallelujah!

Land of conquest, land of peace, Praise the Lord!

We have reach'd the happy shore, Hallelujah!

We shall live in sin no more, Praise the Lord!

O How Sad to Have Lived

(also known as "The Harvest Is Past")

Verse 1

O how sad to have lived as did Israel of old,

In a land where Jehovah is known,

With His good word to guide us to glories untold,

And make us bright heirs to the throne,

And still to neglect His way to pursue,

And drive His good Spirit away:

Yes, stubbornly fail his commandments to do,

Till we, too, like Israel shall say:

Refrain

The harvest is past, the summer is ended,

And we are not saved;

The harvest is past, the summer is ended,

And we are not saved.

Verse 2

Brother, what shall we say when the Lord shall withdraw,

And seek us in mercy no more?

When his good Spirit griev'd that we love not His law,

Shall no longer knock at the door?

Oh, what shall we plead, oh, how shall we do

When mercy and truth shall depart?

'Twere vain then to rise and the Lord to pursue;

Oh, list to that desolate heart:

Verse 3

When at last we shall see that the Bible is true,

And we have rejected its light,

Oh, tell me, dear brother, what then shall we do,

When Judgment is rolling in sight?

When Nineveh stands with the Sodom of old,

Condemning the men of this day,

When those who lived godly shall enter the fold,

Oh, brother, what then shall we say?

Verse 4

O how sad to look back on the deeds we have done,

On the words of unkindness we've said,

On the vows yet unkept, and the privilege gone,

Before us eternity dread!

How sad then to meet the Savior we scorn

In order to walk with the world!

Oh, then shall we wish we had never been born,

As downward to death we are hurled!

The Strong Man Bound

Verse 1

Jesus the strong man was bound for us all,

Jesus is mighty to save;

Jesus will save us if on Him we call,

Jesus is mighty to save.

Refrain

Jesus is mighty to save;

Jesus has conquered death, hell, and the grave;

Jesus gives vic'try to all who believe,

Jesus is mighty to save.

Verse 2

Jesus the price of our ransom has paid,

Jesus is mighty to save;

Full, free atonement for all He has made,

Jesus is mighty to save.

Verse 3

Conquering grace unto all He will give,

Jesus is mighty to save;

If we to please Him are willing to live,

Jesus is mighty to save.

Verse 4

O do not doubt Him, nor limit His power,

Jesus is mighty to save;

Let not the threats of the foe make you cower,

Jesus is mighty to save.

Verse 5

Trust Him and try Him, O brother, and see,

Jesus is mighty to save;

Plenteous redemption He's promised to thee,

Jesus is mighty to save.

There's Coming a Time

Verse 1

There's coming a time when all who have
      journeyed patiently in the heavenly way,
Will hear the dear Master tenderly saying,
      "Enter my rest, O child of the day."

Refrain

Will you be one? O will you be one?
Will you be there, your life's work all done?
As the redeemed shall hear the glad welcome?

Verse 1

There's coming a time of judgment eternal,
      day when the works of men shall be tried:
When only the pure, the godly, the holy,
      happy with Christ in heav'n shall abide.

Verse 1

There's coming a time when sinners shall hear
      Him, saying in anger, "From me depart!"
And driven to doom, shall wail that they never
      gave to the Lord the love of their heart.

Verse 1

This wonderful time is swiftly approaching —
      will you not now to meet it prepare?
Repent and believe, be filled with the Spirit;
      Hurry! The time of judgment is near.

Precious Savior

Verse 1

Precious Savior, I implore Thee, all thy fullness now impart;

Keep thy love-wings hovered o'er me, dwell Thyself within my heart.

Precious Savior, precious Savior, all my treasure Lord, Thou art.

Verse 2

Let not sin again defile me, keep me holy, faithful, pure:

Never from Thy face exile me, love me, keep me evermore.

In Thy favor, in Thy favor, my poor longing heart assure.

Verse 3

Hide me from the world's alluring, buried with Thee into death;

Let me, all life's ills enduring, walk the holy way of faith.

Precious Savior, precious Savior, keep me in the narrow path.

C. P. Jones's Instructions on Making Church Music

This set of instructions, mostly focused on choir practice and choir members, shows the breadth of Jones's concern as a musician. Not only was he busily composing new pieces during his Jackson ministry; he was also concerned about the quality of music his choir produced and the preparation necessary for the same. In this section of instructions, copyrighted in 1902, Jones is eager to exhort choir members to be engaged fully with both their hearts and their minds, yet to avoid affectation or "put on," which is "objectionable to all refined people."

One of the mysteries about Jones is where he received training to write the music which accompanies his lyrics. Was it in his own college program or by association with someone at Jackson College? No one knows for sure.

INDUCTIVE LESSONS IN VOCAL MUSIC

(a) Unless there is music in one, it is hard to get it out with ever so much training; yet one does not know what he can do until he tries.

(b) "I will sing with the spirit and with the understanding also," said the inspired apostle; which showed that he believed in correct singing, but in the spirit of devotion as well. The heart of the church choir should be prepared for singing as the heart of the minister is prepared for his sermon.

(c) "Be at peace among yourselves" would do admirably well as a choir motto, and with it such blessed divine instruction as "Let all your things be done in charity" (1 Cor. 16:14). "In honor preferring one another" (Rom. 12:10). "Do all to the glory of God" (1 Cor. 10:31).

(d) While the singing practice need not be a funeral occasion, it should not be either an occasion of folly and fuss. God is present with His people everywhere; learn to "practice the thought of His presence," and respect Him.

(e) Sing full, round tones. Do not blare like a file against a saw. If the voice at first be not sweet and musical, practice will bring it to be so. To this end, sing much when by yourself. Practice the scale; practice correct pronunciation. Yet so practice it as to let your heart be on what you sing, not how. Avoid any sort of "put on."

(f) Do not sound R in words where there is no R. That is affectation or put on, and is objectionable to all refined people.

The concern for being properly "refined people" is another marker for Christ Temple's place within the spectrum of Christian worship.

(g) Give all words their proper sound as nearly as can be done in singing. Teacher, see to this; but do not criticize to the point of discouraging your pupil.

(h) Do not be late to choir practice — only when compelled. Then be polite enough to render excuse and beg pardon.

(i) Why should you be late at the service, either? God, the Spirit, needs your help. Render it to Him so soon as you can. Good singing done by willing hearts and trained minds and voices is such help. In Solomon's temple, certain of the Levites were especially appointed to this service. You have somewhat their place. Be humble and diligent and fill it well (2 Chron. 5:12-14).

(j) Practice so much to yourself that you can sing well at sight, but don't become puffed about it; that would take all the virtue and power out of an otherwise useful accomplishment.

(k) Do not be afraid to sing with rejoicing. Fastidiousness spoils much of the joy of life. Let us love God, love souls, love music — and sing. That's what we are here for — to sing! (Isa. 12). Many a soul has been converted by a song, and many a despairing one filled with renewed hope. We can live life but once; then, filled with the spirit of God's own holiness, let us do our best and sing.

(l) Get you a dictionary and learn what words which you don't know mean, so that you may be thorough and both study and sing with the understanding as well as with the spirit. Do not be too lazy to know. Ask those who know to help you. Expose your ignorance, if need be, and acquire knowledge. Do this and see how it will profit you in days to come.

Such phrases as "politeness to your Maker and Redeemer" show that Jones's concern is not only the passion or ecstasy that can be stimulated by worship.

(m) Invoke God's help in all things. Let your knowledge thus be sanctified and pay the debt of politeness to your Maker and Redeemer.

(n) In studying these lessons, notice well the parts in larger type. Don't leave them till you get the sense of what is said so that you can give it in your own words. Let your mind master something; it will do you good. Whether people seem to appreciate it right away or not, they will someday.

(o) But sing; nothing will teach how to do this like doing. "Have grace and sing" (Heb. 12:28-29).

II.

Let us now proceed to study vocal music.

It appears that Jones intended the church's music to be approached with the same studiousness he expected for all of life.

Observe, however, that this is not an exhaustive treatise on the subject, but it will give one sufficient knowledge to be a fairly intelligent reader of music. And the songbook with this treatise is especially adapted to the purpose.

What follows in the original is an introduction to basic music theory, which is why it's not included here.

Source: C. P. Jones, *Jesus Only, Nos. 1 and 2 Combined* (Bogalusa, La.: R. C. Cook for the National Publishing Board of the Church of Christ, Holiness, 1935). Along with Jones's autobiographical sketch and the history of his songs, this piece can be found in the *Journal of Black Sacred Music* 2 (Fall 1988): 81-82.

A Special Worship Program for Easter

C. P. Jones designed the following service, published in 1913, as a Sunday school exercise for children. Note its didactic quality as it seeks to instruct the children in the facts and meaning of Christ's resurrection. Jones composed much of the material for the exercise, including the ingenious poetical catechism framed as a boy/girl dialogue. Such pieces illustrate how much the fledgling church used the creative output of its founding minister in worship. At times the program merely mentions a prayer and other things that would have been done extemporaneously, leaving no paper trail on important practices for historians.

EASTER PROGRAM FOR SUNDAY SCHOOL

(We insert this program in order that it may be used or that it may serve as a model to any desiring to get up an Easter service among children.)

March 23, 1913

1. Song. "Praise God, from Whom all Blessings Flow."
2. Prayer. (Standing after singing.)
3. Bible Reading, Romans, 6th chapter, led by someone appointed by the Superintendent.
4. Song. "Grace to Die." *(Jesus Only)*
5. Bible Reading. Matthew, 28th chapter.
6. Song. "They Crucified My Savior." *(Sweet Selections)*[27]
7. Recitation:

"He Rose."

He rose, the Son of David rose
Eternal secrets to disclose,
To open Hell's barred gates, and free
From Death's dominions you and me.

He rose. The Jews said He would not,
And Roman soldiers kept the spot

"Grace to Die" records Jesus' statement about denial and taking up the cross for those who wish to follow him.

"They Crucified My Savior" tells the story of Jesus' resurrection, starting with his crucifixion and burial. Each verse highlights a different event in this biblical story.

---

27. *Jesus Only* and *Sweet Selections* refer to different song collections that Jones had published.

Where He was buried, night and day,
That none might steal His corpse away.

He rose, for angels came from heaven
And shook the earth like thunder seven,
Broke Rome's proud seal, rolled back the stone,
And made the grave give up God's Son.

He rose that we be justified,
He rose that we be sanctified,
He rose that we might, too, arise
And claim dominion in the skies.

This hymn connects the saving aspects of Jesus' death, resurrection, and ascension to his return at the end of the ages.

He rose. He who believes this truth,
Learned or ignorant, aged or youth,
Finds in it everlasting peace,
And lives where pleasures never cease.

C. P. Jones

8.   Song. "Jesus Is Coming Again." *(Sweet Selections)*
9.   Children's Dialogue (Boys and Girls): What Happened?

(Dialogue for Easter. Let a number of Boys and Girls recite it standing, one questioning, the other answering. It would be better to let all the boys ask the questions in concert and all the girls answer in the same manner.)

C. P. Jones

Boys. Who was it crucified to be,
    A Savior unto you and me?

Girls. Jesus, God's only Son, who came,
    To save us for His holy name.

Boys. Who buried Him? And tell me where
    They laid His body with such care.

Girls. Joseph and Nicodemus, they,
    In Joseph's tomb laid Him away.

Boys. Who said He would not rise again,
    To have dominion over men?

Girls. The Jews His message did despise,
    And said that He would never rise.

Boys. Whom did they set to watch the grave?

Girls. Some Roman soldiers fierce and brave.

Boys. What happened on a Sunday morn,
    Almost before daylight was born?

Girls. Two angels down from heaven came,
    Their faces with God's light aflame,
    Shook the whole earth, rolled back the stone,
    And Christ came forth the Risen One.

Boys. What happened to the soldiers then?

Girls. They trembled and fell as dead men.

Boys. What story were they paid to tell,
    The truth from mankind to conceal?

Girls. That while they slept (they were to say),
    Christ's followers stole the corpse away.

Boys. But who saw Jesus after then?

Girls. O, more than half a thousand men.

Boys. What woman saw Him first, cause she
    Went early there her Lord to see?

Girls. Why Mary Magdalene came,

    First to the tomb, He called her name.

    The other women saw Him then;

    They went there earlier than the men.

Boys. Where is our risen Lord today?

Girls. Up in the heavens far away.

Boys. What is He doing over there?

Girls. He keeps engaged for us in prayer.

Boys. And shall we e'er His sweet face see?

Girls. Yes, if we serve Him faithfully.

10.   Select Reading. 1 Cor., 15th chapter.
11.   Solo. "It Was Early" (or some other selection)
12.   Chorus. "O That Land." *(Sweet Selections)*
13.   Examination of the School on the knowledge of Christ and His resurrection.

(1)   What type do we get in Genesis of Christ's resurrection? Isaac. (Tell about it.)

(2)   What in the law of Moses? The scapegoat who bore sin away while the other goat (or sin offering) died for sin.[28]

(3)   Who among the prophets? Jonah, who was three days and three nights in the whale's belly.[29]

(4)   What sign of it have we in gospel ceremonies? The baptism of Jesus and our own baptism. Matthew 3, Romans 6, Colossians 2.

(5)   What doctrine does it set forth? That we are risen with Christ to justification of life. (Rom. 4:24-25; explain)

(6)   What else? It is a guarantee that we who believe in Him shall walk holy before Him and at last enjoy the resurrection of the body.

14.   Scripture recitations by children.
15.   Song. "We Are Pilgrims." *(Sweet Selections)*

28. See Leviticus 16:8ff.
29. In Matthew 12:40, Jesus compares his own death and resurrection to the experience of Jonah.

"It was Early" recounts the opening events of Christ's resurrection. Like many of the pieces in this program, that specific event is tied to both justification and sanctification, the two great dimensions of salvation in a Holiness theology. "O That Land" celebrates the Christian hope of arriving safely in heaven.

Jones probably has in mind the story in Genesis 22 of Abraham being commanded to sacrifice Isaac. Compare Hebrews 11:19, which states that Abraham did receive Isaac back from the dead, figuratively speaking.

"We Are Pilgrims" celebrates the church's joyous arrival to its heavenly home. It is another way that Jones connects the resurrection to larger themes of salvation.

16.   Recitation. "Passing."

17.   Song. "O Sinner, Where Will You Stand?" *(Jesus Only* & *Sweet Selections)*

18.   Call for professions of Christ.

19.   Announcements.

20.   Benediction.

Source: Charles P. Jones, *Sermons of Life and Power* (Jackson, Miss.: Truth Publishing Co., 1913; reprint, National Publishing Board, Church of Christ [Holiness] U.S.A., 2004), pp. 137-40.

The emergence of special calls at the end of services to make a public profession or come to a designated spot like an altar has been a part of Christian worship since altar calls as such became a part of American evangelicalism in the late 18th century.

Texts for Sacraments, Weddings, and Funerals

The following liturgical texts are from the denomination's earliest polity book, the Manual of the History, Doctrine, Government, and Ritual of the Church of Christ (Holiness) U.S.A., 1926. *(Charles Price Jones was not on the editorial committee of the Manual.) In the book the church adopted an episcopal church government (i.e., the church recognized bishops to lead it); not surprisingly, the texts below show the direct influence of other episcopal denominations' resources, like the rites and ceremonies for the African Methodist Episcopal Church. The influence is especially strong in the marriage and funeral texts. The baptismal and communion texts, in contrast, show less dependence, possibly reflecting older sensibilities from Baptist or other roots.*

RITUAL

I. BAPTISM

II. RECEPTION OF MEMBERS

III. THE LORD'S SUPPER

IV. MATRIMONY

V. BURIAL SERVICE

Chapter I. Baptism

With the candidates standing at the pool:

Beloved of the Lord: Believing that God for Christ's sake has forgiven you for your sins, and that you are saved by grace through faith, and that you are prepared to put on Christ by baptism, you will further avow the same by answering the following questions.

Do you believe in God, the Father Almighty, Maker of heaven and earth, and in Jesus Christ, His only begotten Son, our Lord? That He was conceived by the Holy Ghost, born of the Virgin Mary? That He suffered under Pontius Pilate, was crucified, dead, and buried? That the third day He arose from the dead? That He ascended into heaven, and sitteth at the right hand of God the Father Almighty, and from thence shall come again to judge the quick and the dead? And do you believe in the Holy Ghost? The Church of Christ? The communion of saints? The remission of sins? The resurrection of the dead? And the life everlasting?

Using the creed in a question-and-answer format at the time of baptism is an ancient practice.

Answer: All this I do believe.

Do you renounce the world, flesh, and the devil, to walk with Jesus?

Answer: I do. (Prayer and song)

The Minister shall then take the candidates one by one into the pool and say:

On the confession of your faith, and in obedience to our Lord's command, I baptize thee in the name of the Father, and of the Son, and of the Holy Ghost, Amen.

Chapter II. Reception of Members

On receiving members into the church before baptism.

Beloved of the Lord: We read in Rom. 10:9-10 that if thou shalt confess with thy mouth the Lord Jesus, and shalt believe in thine heart that God hath raised Him from the dead, thou shalt be saved. For with the heart man believeth unto righteousness; and with the mouth confession is made unto salvation.

Do you believe that you are converted?

Answer: I do.

Are you willing to confess when and wherever it need be, that you are converted?

The dual emphasis of Holiness thought can be seen in these questions: members must affirm both justification (conversion) and sanctification. Notice that the rite calls only for an experience of conversion, not sanctification, for membership.

Answer: I am willing.

Do you believe in sanctification?

Answer: I do.

Are you willing to obey all of the rules of government of the Church of Christ (Holiness) U.S.A.?

Answer: I am willing.

The pastor or the person acting in the pastor's place will then receive them by vote of the Church.

The above questions will be all that are necessary in taking a person into the Church.

After baptism, just before giving communion, with the candidates facing the audience, [the minister speaks] to the congregation:

Dearly Beloved: In the Sixteenth Chapter of Romans we are taught the outflow of Christian love. In the sixteenth verse of this same chapter, we read, "the Churches of Christ salute you."

In the sixteenth chapter of the Gospel according to St. Matthew, beginning with the thirteenth verse, we read: "When Jesus came into the coasts of Caesarea Philippi, He asked His disciples, saying, 'Whom do men say that I, the Son of Man, am?' And they said, 'Some say that thou art John the Baptist; some, Elias; and others, Jeremiah, or one of the prophets.' He saith unto them, 'But whom say ye that I am?'

"And Simon Peter answered and said, 'Thou art the Christ, the Son of the living God.' And Jesus answered and said unto him, 'Blessed art thou, Simon Bar-jona: for flesh and blood hath not revealed it unto thee, but my Father which is in heaven. And I say also unto thee, that thou art Peter, and upon this rock I will build my Church; and the gates of hell shall not prevail against it.' "

The minister shall then say to the candidates:

With pleasure we recognize you as members of the Church of Christ, and bid you welcome to all its privileges; and in token of our brotherly love, we give you the right hand of fellowship, and pray that you may be numbered with his people here, and in heaven.

The minister shall then say to the congregation:

Brethren, I commend to your love, care, and keeping these persons whom we this day recognize as members of the Church of Christ.

Do all in your power to increase their faith, confirm their hope, and perfect them in love. (Let us pray.)

Then shall follow a hymn suitable to the occasion, while the congregation shakes hands with the candidates.

CHAPTER III. THE LORD'S SUPPER

The sermon being over and the collection taken, the Pastor, Ministers, and Officers shall gather near the communion table. Someone may sing while this is being done. After which the minister will say:

For I have received of the Lord that which also I delivered unto you, That the Lord Jesus the same night in which he was betrayed took bread:

And when He had given thanks, He broke it, and said, "Take, eat: this is my body, which is broken for you: this do in remembrance of me."

After the same manner also he took the cup, when he had supped, saying, "This cup is the new testament in my blood: this do ye, as oft as ye drink it, in remembrance of me. For as often as ye eat this bread, and drink this cup, ye do show the Lord's death till he come.

"Wherefore whosoever shall eat this bread, and drink this cup of the Lord, unworthily, shall be guilty of the body and blood of the Lord.

"But let a man examine himself, and so let him eat of that bread, and drink of that cup.

"For he that eateth and drinketh unworthily, eateth and drinketh damnation to himself, not discerning the Lord's body.

"Wherefore, my brethren, when you come together to eat, tarry one for another.

"And if any man hunger, let him eat at home; that ye come not together unto condemnation. And the rest will I set in order when I come."

The Communion service is very short and straightforward, reflecting perhaps Baptist roots. The text itself is taken from the King James Version of 1 Corinthians 11:23ff. Notice that the account of the sacrament's institution is given as an address to the congregation, not as part of a prayer of thanksgiving. The older Christian tradition is to include it as the culminating remembrance as part of a longer recitation of God's saving activity in a prayer of thanksgiving.

Then shall follow a prayer of consecration over the bread and wine, after which the Minister, himself partaking with the other Ministers present, and then the Officers of the Church, and then the people.

The Minister, when passing the communion, will say:

(THE BREAD)

The body of our Lord Jesus Christ, which was broken for thee: take and eat this in remembrance that Christ died for thee.

(THE WINE)

The blood of our Lord Jesus Christ, which was shed for thee.

The communion may be passed to the people by the officer of the church.

After which let everybody shake hands and pass out [of the church].

Chapter IV. Matrimony

At the time and place appointed for the solemnization of Matrimony, the persons to be married, having been qualified according to law, standing together, the man on the right hand and the woman on the left, the Minister shall say:

Dearly Beloved: We are gathered together here in the sight of God, and in the presence of these witnesses, to join together this man and this woman in holy wedlock, which is an honorable estate, instituted of God in the time of man's innocence, signifying unto us the mystical union that exists between Christ and His Church; which holy estate Christ adorned and beautified with His presence and first miracle that He wrought, in Cana of Galilee. The Scriptures teach us that it is honorable among all men; therefore it is to be entered into wisely, reverently, discreetly, and in the fear of God.

Into which holy estate these persons present come now to be joined. Therefore, if any can show just cause why they may not lawfully be joined together, let him now speak, or else for ever hold his peace.

The Minister shall then say to the persons that are to be married:

I charge you both, that if either of you know any impediment why you may not be lawfully joined together in matrimony, you do now confess it; for be you well assured that so many as are joined together otherwise than God's Word doth allow, are not joined together by the Lord, neither is their Matrimony lawful.

There being no impediment, then shall the Minister say unto the man:

Wilt thou have this woman to be thy wedded wife, to live together after God's ordinance in the holy estate of Matrimony? Wilt thou love her, comfort her, honor and keep her, in sickness and in health; and, forsaking all others, keep thee only unto her, so long as ye both shall live?

The man shall answer:

I will.

Then shall the Minister say unto the woman:

Among Christian worship services, the words of the wedding service are some of the best known. Why might that be?

Wilt thou have this man to be thy wedded husband, to live together after God's ordinance in the holy estate of Matrimony? Wilt thou love, honor, and keep him in sickness and in health; and, forsaking all others, keep thee only unto him, so long as you both shall live?

The woman shall answer:

I will.

If there is a ring, the Minister will give the ring to the man, to put it on the third finger of the woman's left hand; and the man, holding the ring there, will repeat after the Minister:

This service has made a significant omission at this point — namely, the wedding vows themselves ("I, N——, take thee, N——, to be my wedded. . . ."). The reason for the omission is not clear.

With this ring I thee wed, and with all my worldly goods I thee endow: in the name of the Father, and of the Son, and of the Holy Ghost. Amen.

If there be no ring, the Minister will pray:

O Eternal God, Creator and Preserver of all mankind, Giver of all spiritual grace, the Author of everlasting life, send Thy blessing upon these Thy servants, this man and this woman, whom we bless in Thy name; that, as Isaac and Rebecca lived faithfully together, so these persons may surely perform and keep the vow and covenant between them made, and may ever remain in perfect love and peace together, and live according to Thy laws: through Jesus Christ our Lord. Amen.

Then shall the Minister join their right hands together, and say:

Forasmuch as this man and this woman have consented together in holy wedlock, and have witnessed the same before God and this company, and have declared the same by joining of hands, I pronounce that they are husband and wife together, and in the name of the Father, and of the Son, and of the Holy Ghost. Those whom God hath joined together let no man put asunder. Amen.

The Minister shall add his blessing:

God, the Father, the Son, and the Holy Ghost, bless, preserve, and keep you; the Lord mercifully with His favor look upon you, and so fill you with all spiritual benediction and grace, that you may so live together in this life that in the world to come ye may have life everlasting. Amen.

Chapter V. Burial Service

The Minister, meeting the corpse at the door, and going down the aisle before it, shall say:

Like many funeral services, this text starts with a strong promise from God. Its beneficial quality is obvious in a funeral. In a regular worship service, how quickly should God get a good "first word"?

I am the resurrection and the life: he that believeth in me, though he were dead, yet shall he live; and whosoever liveth, and believeth in me, shall never die. I know that my Redeemer liveth, and that He shall stand at the latter day upon the earth; and though after my skin, worms destroy this body, yet in my flesh shall I see God: whom I shall see for myself, and mine eyes shall behold, and not another. We brought nothing into this world, and it is certain we can carry nothing out. The Lord giveth, and the Lord hath taken away: blessed be the name of the Lord.

After coming into the Church, or house, then shall be read, after everybody is seated, and the first song sung:

Lord, thou hast been our dwelling place in all generations.

Before the mountains were brought forth, or ever thou hadst formed the earth and world, even from everlasting to everlasting, thou art God.

Thou turnest man to destruction; and sayest, Return, ye children of men.

For a thousand years in thy sight are but as yesterday when it is past, and as a watch in the night.

Thou carriest them away as with a flood; they are as a sleep: in the morning they are like a grass which groweth up.

In the morning it flourisheth, and groweth up; in the evening it is cut down and withereth.

For we are consumed by thine anger, and by thy wrath are we troubled.

Thou hast set our iniquities before thee, our secret sins in the light of thy countenance.

For all our days are passed away in thy wrath: we spend our years as a tale that is told.

The days of our years are threescore years and ten; and if by reason of strength they be fourscore years, yet is their strength, labor, and sorrow; for it is soon cut off, and we fly away.

Who knoweth the power of thine anger? Even according to thy fear, so is thy wrath.

So teach us to number our days, that we may apply our hearts unto wisdom.

Return, O Lord, how long? And let it repent thee concerning thy servants.

O satisfy us early with thy mercy; that we may rejoice and be glad all our days. Make us glad according to the days wherein thou hast afflicted us, and the years wherein we have seen evil.

Let thy work appear unto thy servants, and thy glory unto their children.

And let the beauty of the Lord our God be upon us; and establish thou the work of our hands upon us; the work of our hands establish thou it (Psalm XC).

The text comes from Psalm 90. Finding the right words in worship is not always easy, particularly in times of distress or trouble. Christians over the centuries have shown a predilection for using the Psalms as a prayer book for the church.

Then shall follow the prayer and whatever is to be had before the sermon, and then the sermon.

After the sermon, and reviewing of the remains; in the Church, or at the grave, when the corpse is laid in the earth, the Minister shall say:

Man that is born of a woman is of a few days, and full of trouble. He cometh forth like a flower, and is cut down; he fleeth also as a shadow, and continueth not.

In the midst of life we are in death: of whom may we seek for succor, but of thee, O Lord, who for our sins art justly displeased?

Yet, O Lord God most Holy, deliver us not unto the bitter pains of eternal death.

Then the Minister will say:

For as much as it hath pleased Almighty God to take out of this world the soul of our deceased brother, we therefore commit his body to the ground, earth to earth, ashes to ashes, dust to dust; looking for the general resurrection in the last day, and life of the world to come, through our Lord Jesus Christ; at whose second coming in glorious majesty to judge the world, the earth and the sea shall give up their dead; and the corruptible bodies of those who sleep in him shall be changed, and made like unto his own glorious body, according to the mighty working where he is able to subdue all things unto himself.

Then may follow the Lord's Prayer, or the following benediction:

The grace of the Lord Jesus Christ, and the love of God, and the communion of the Holy Ghost be with you all. Amen.

If the corpse is a child, read 2 Sam. 12:15-23, instead of Psalm 90.

Source: *Manual of the History, Doctrine, Government, and Ritual of the Church of Christ (Holiness) U.S.A., 1926* (Norfolk, Va.: Guide Publishing Co., 1926).

Sermons

C. P. Jones's Sermon on the Baptism of the Spirit

In the following sermon, C. P. Jones highlighted how critical the Holy Spirit was for the Christian believer and for the church. The sermon reflects tensions between the Holiness and Pentecostal movements in the early twentieth century. For example, notice how Jones was careful to define what he meant by the biblical phrase "baptism of the Holy Ghost," which was an important technical term in both movements. Likewise, Jones clearly noted the points at which he thought Pentecostal doctrine on the Spirit had gone awry: systematizing the baptism of the Holy Ghost as a culminating experience in a line of spiritual experiences (conversion/justification, sanctification/anointing, and then this baptism) and making speaking in tongues required evidence of having received the baptism of the Holy Ghost.

This sermon and the two others below were published by C. P. Jones sometime after they were preached. It's hard to know exactly what they would have sounded like when they were preached, since printing mutes a sermon's oral quality.

THE GIFT OF THE HOLY GHOST

The Gospel dispensation is called "the ministration of the Spirit" (2 Cor. 3:7-8). Jesus went away, having fully completed the atonement, having taken away sin by the sacrifice of Himself, that the Comforter might come. He in coming was to convince the world of sin, of righteousness, and of judgment to come, and to guide the believer into all truth. This is Christ's epitome, our Savior's own summing up of the dispensation and work of the Holy Spirit. The Savior in this wonderful dispensational administration of the Spirit thoroughly and personally identifies Himself with the Holy Spirit, as the following passages show:

> "If ye love Me, ye will keep My commandments.
>
> And I will pray the Father, and He shall give you another Comforter, that He may be with you forever.
>
> Even the Spirit of truth: whom the world cannot receive; for it beholdeth Him not, neither knoweth Him; but ye know Him; for He abideth with you, and shall be in you.
>
> I will never leave you desolate: I come unto you.
>
> Yet a little while, and the world beholdeth Me no more, but ye behold Me: because I live, ye shall live also.
>
> In that day ye shall know that I am in My Father, and ye in Me, and I in you."
>
> John 14:15-20

Jones's strong devotional attachment to Jesus Christ is reinforced by this sort of close connection between Christ and the Holy Spirit.

Jones switches between calling the Third Person of the Trinity the Holy Spirit and the Holy Ghost. He likely does so because the King James Version of the Bible likewise uses both terms. See 1 Corinthians 12:3, where both are used.

"Now the Lord is the Spirit: and where the Spirit of the Lord is, there is liberty.

But we all, with unveiled face, beholding as in a mirror the glory of the Lord, are transformed into the same image from glory to glory, even as from the Lord the Spirit."

2 Cor. 3:17-18

Our Savior and the Spirit are one. The Holy Spirit is Christ at work in the world saving men in His divine, invisible, omnipresent, and almighty aspect. In Romans, eighth chapter, the statement "If any man have not the Spirit of Christ, he is none of His" is followed by the statement "If Christ be in you, the body is dead because of sin, but the Spirit is life because of righteousness" [Rom. 10:9-10].

IN THE BOOK OF ACTS

Jesus Began — Jesus Continues

This throws light on the statement made in the text, "Of all that Jesus began both to do and to teach." Indeed, as our propitiation, as our sacrifice and officiating high priest, He completed, finished — yes, perfected forever — His work; as teacher of men, administrator of the will of God, and Savior of the world, He only began His work when He was personally here in the flesh. He is to carry it on in the person of the Holy Ghost. The work of Jesus Christ, the son of Mary, endued with the Holy Ghost, is given us in the four records made by Matthew, Mark, Luke, and John. The record of Christ Jesus and the Holy Spirit (see Rom. 8:8-9; Acts 16:7; 2 Cor. 3:17-18; and Revelation, chapters 1, 2, & 3) is given in the book of Acts; how [by] enduing His church with His own power, filling it with and baptizing it in His own presence, and imparting to it His own love, zeal, wisdom, and holiness, He continued the work many years. In the same Holy Spirit He will continue this work till He comes again. Phil. 1:6; Heb. 13:20.

The Church Is God at Work

As God was in Christ reconciling the world unto Himself, He is in the church doing the same thing. This is clear from 1 Corinthians, twelfth chapter, where the baptism of the Holy Spirit as an abiding blessing is explained as it is nowhere else. To understand this chapter is to get much rest and blessing, and will save from terrible delusions and fanatical mistakes. Yet, only those who are taught of the Lord by the Spirit will ever understand God. This is clear from 1 Corinthians, second chapter.

Jesus bade His disciples to wait for the promise of the Father. This promise, it is made clear from the text, was the baptism, outpouring, coming upon, receiving gift or enduement of the Holy Ghost.

Figures of Speech

Any student of Acts can see that our Savior's real aim was to get the church to be still till He could come back and fill her with Himself in the Holy Spirit because He is both the power of God and the wisdom of God. 1 Cor. 1:24. To convert a man takes divine power, to sanctify a man takes divine power. To take care of the church takes wisdom divine; to understand God, to appreciate Him, takes a divine revelation in the soul. It took the Holy Spirit to make Christ of quick understanding in the fear of the Lord (Isa. 11:1-11), that He might recover His remnant.

The baptism of the Holy Ghost therefore expresses the divine presence in and upon the church, empowering her for her work. Sanctifying her in God, making her wise unto salvation, and sealing her as the bride of Christ. 1 John 2:20-27; Eph. 1:13; 4:30.

But remember that only three times do Christ and the apostles refer to the Holy Spirit's presence as a baptism — twice in the book of Acts, once in 1 Corinthians, 12th chapter. His presence is also called the gift of the Holy Ghost. As a gift to us, He is referred to most. In John 7:37-39, John 14:16, Acts 2:38 and 5:32, and a number of other passages, He is referred to as a gift, as given unto us. And surely He is a gift to us. He was not in any such sense a gift to the prophets as He is to us. To them He was given occasionally because they were leaders of the people. Now, as the birthright of all, He is the gift of Christ to every believer's heart who will receive Him.

> Both of these assertions would be rejections of Pentecostal teaching. Jones seems to be saying that the "baptism" of the Holy Spirit has a communal emphasis — rather than an individual one — and that even the language itself is not that common and thus should not be that important.

But of the meaning of these other figures in Acts by which the gift of the Spirit is known, we want to speak in other discourses. Now we want to speak of the term "the baptism of the Spirit" and what is implied in it.

Two Events

We find the term "baptism of the Spirit" mentioned in the record of two events, the day of Pentecost and the case of Cornelius. In both cases the blessing was called an outpouring. In the one case He was outpoured on people some of whom had received the Spirit and been illuminated before. Now they seem to have received a larger infilling and empowering. With others it was their first experience. Yet we never hear of what is now preached to us in some quarters that we are converted or justified, then receive sanctification or an anointing, then go on and "get the baptism of the Holy Ghost." Nowhere in the Acts or the epistles is such a process described, though we do see that the Ephesians, after having received the Spirit, were prayed for, that they might be strengthened with might by the Spirit in the inner man; and they are yet exhorted to be "filled with the Spirit" [Eph. 3:16; 5:18]. But this is not put as if they had received an anointing at first and must now receive their baptism, their Pentecost. There are deeper depths, even all the fullness of God, but it all belongs in the ministry of the Spirit

> These three stages of experience reflect some early Pentecostal thought that Jones rejects. His point is that deeper experiences of the Spirit are possible — even desirable — but we shouldn't designate them by biblical terms or standardize them into a system.

Jones's basic point is clear: Pentecostal teachers are not scriptural.

Having repudiated early Pentecostal thought on the baptism of the Holy Spirit, Jones must offer what he considers a sounder, more scriptural definition. He begins by looking closely at the account of the original Pentecost in Acts 2.

and is not called the baptism of the Spirit. It is best to be literally scriptural, or else the scriptural man is in danger of going mad — "The spiritual man is mad," said the prophet [Hos. 9:7], foreshadowing without doubt our days of delusions and false propagandas. And yet are not many of these the efforts of honest men to get out of the scriptures all that is in them? The only safe path is to be literally, strictly, jealously scriptural to the law and the testimony.[30] If they speak not according to this word, it is because there is NO LIGHT IN THEM.

What It Means

What does baptism mean? It means an overwhelming, a submersion, an immersion, a burial. And what happened on the day of Pentecost? The room was filled with the presence of the Spirit, He having come as with the sound of a mighty, rushing wind. We have been in many a room so filled with His presence that it seemed to us we could almost see Him. At no other time is it recorded in the Bible that He came with such a sound. Tongues of fire sat on those who were present. At no other time did this occur, that we know of. Yet we know when those who have seen the minister lost in the Spirit have seen, as they said, a flaming light upon him.

It pleased the Holy Spirit to manifest Himself also by giving certain miraculous gifts to the disciples on this as on other similar occasions. They began to speak with other tongues "as the Spirit gave them utterance." It is to be remarked that all were filled; it is not said that all spake with tongues. Yet all might have done so had it so pleased the Spirit; for all power is in Him. To manifest Himself with one gift is as easy as to manifest Himself with another. Blessed be He!

The Greek here is *Kai epleestheesan pantes pneumatos hagiou, Kai eerxanto lalein heterais glossais kathos to pnuema edidon apophtheggesthai autois.* "And they were all filled with the Holy Spirit, and they began to speak with other tongues, as the Spirit gave them utterance." "They BEGAN to speak with tongues" carries a different idea from "they all DID speak with tongues." We object not to the Spirit's so manifesting Himself at any time; we only would not have Him misrepresented and so exalt a gift above the Lord Himself. For as the scriptures are being strained and misinterpreted in certain quarters, a false doctrine is gone abroad, giving place to the devil and greatly deluding earnest souls.

The great, the mighty fact of the day of Pentecost was that all were FILLED WITH THE SPIRIT and were overwhelmed in Him. They in God, God in them. He, the Spirit, made them conscious of that. O glorious consciousness, that we are in God and God in us! We know it because "God is love, and he that dwells in love dwells in God and God in him." We know it because "God is light, and in Him is no darkness at all."

While Jones's use of Greek here is unexceptional for many today, it must be understood as remarkable in context. Jones was less than a year away from having been born into slavery. And during his adult ministry, Jim Crow laws and other forms of racial oppression still marked the majority's attitude toward African-Americans. And yet not only is Jones educated at a basic level; he can also engage in detailed exegesis of the Bible in its original language.

30. See Isaiah 8:20. Protestants have sometimes used "the law and the testimony" to refer to the whole of Scripture.

Cornelius' Case

The only other time the gift of the Spirit is called a baptism is in the book of Acts in the case of Cornelius. Here, too, the blessing is called an outpouring. Here, too, is a crowd "all of one mind," though they have not been clearly converted till the same sermon under which they are filled. The inference seems clear that where a large number are filled with the Spirit at once, and He at the same time falls without the laying on of hands — [this] is called an outpouring or baptism. From the twelfth chapter of First Corinthians we see that the gift of the Spirit to the church as a whole is so-called — "baptized by [Greek "in"] one Spirit into one body, whether we be Jews or Gentiles, whether we be bond or free."

In the case of Cornelius, too, the gift of tongues was bestowed on certain ones but not all. Evidently some spoke with tongues, while others prophesied and prayed and praised. There is no telling in how many ways they magnified God. We know that Mary magnified God without speaking in a foreign language. Yet every man's tongue is new when he is converted, and especially so when he is filled with the Spirit; for "old things are passed away, and all things are become new." 2 Cor. 5:14-17. The language by no means justifies the inference that all speak with tongues. 1 Cor. 12:30-31. The language is, "For they heard them speaking with tongues and glorifying God." The glorifying of God was not necessarily glorifying except in the sense that God is glorified in all men in the Spirit. The justifiable inference of the language is that some spoke with tongues while others shouted "Glory to God!" in the tongue then and there in common use. Praise God for whatever way it pleases Him to manifest Himself. We would not make little of His gifts; we would only calmly and humbly examine the scriptures and get their literal sense, lest through false interpretations we magnify error instead of the Lord and give place to Satan. Again, it comes that those [who] were noted as speaking in tongues there understood were men. Now it is deluded women and irresponsible children mostly. Evidently the day of Pentecost has not returned yet. We pray its return in God's time.

A Certain Truth

One thing is certain: we are told to "be filled with the Spirit." We are to receive the Holy Ghost after we believe, and when He fills us, we know it. He manifests Himself in bearing fruit (Gal. 5:22-23), and such gifts as it pleases Him to give us He giveth — above all, boldness to witness that the Savior dwells within.

"Now if any man have not the Spirit of Christ, He is none of His. And if Christ be in you, the body is dead because of sin, but the Spirit is life because of righteousness." Amen.

The scriptures nowhere say the gift of tongues or some sort of unknown jabber is

Jones repudiates another tenet of early Pentecostalism: speaking in tongues is the necessary evidence of having been filled by the Holy Spirit. Like many non-Pentecostals then and since, Jones is concerned that this emphasis upon tongues actually turns Christians away from a solitary devotion to the Lord Jesus Christ by putting something else at the center of their desires.

As part of a larger argument that the real evidence of the Holy Spirit's presence is any speech that glorifies God, Jones claims with this aside that Pentecostalism's main appeal has been to women and children. The complaint is not a new one. Often those who critique new, more ecstatic forms of worship have insinuated the same thing. Why might this be a recurring complaint against ecstatic Christianity?

Jones lays out another set of scriptural markers for the Spirit's presence: the gifts of the Spirit (love, joy, peace, etc.) and the ability to testify to Christ boldly.

evidence that we are filled or baptized. Stand firm! Be true to the traditions left us by written scripture. It will save in these times.

Source: Charles Price Jones, *The Gift of the Holy Ghost in the Book of Acts,* rev. ed. (Jackson, Miss.: National Publishing Board, Church of Christ [Holiness] U.S.A., 1996), pp. 6-12. The sermons in this reprint edition were originally published starting in 1903 in the church's magazine titled *Truth.*

C. P. Jones's Sermon on How Christ Has Achieved Our Salvation

This sermon shows how C. P. Jones might have preached a basic salvation message focused on the atoning death of Christ. In it he proclaims a moderate doctrine of substitutionary atonement ("God laid our sins on Jesus"). Jones emphasizes our benefit from Christ's redeeming activity. Rather than speak of forgiveness of sins first of all or in isolation, he highlights humanity's status as children of God as well as notes sanctification and cleansing of a person's sinful nature as benefits from Christ's death. With these emphases, Jones reflects his Holiness orientation and should be compared favorably to early Methodists. On a practical level, this emphasis meant that in his preaching, Jones would be comfortable with inviting his listeners to be prayed for to experience either justification/forgiveness or sanctification at the end of a worship service.

CHRIST OUR SIN OFFERING

> "Yet it pleased the Lord to bruise Him: He hath put Him to grief: when thou shalt make His soul an offering for sin, He shall see His seed, He shall prolong His days, and the pleasure of the Lord shall prosper in His hand." Isa. 53:10.

Isaiah, who prophesied about seven hundred years before our Lord groaned on Calvary, saw by prophetic vision a Deliverer coming.

Conditions in Isaiah's day were dark and discouraging in the extreme. Sin had fully corrupted the people. They had been chastened for their iniquities until from the crown of the head to the sole of the foot there was no soundness in them, social, religious, business, or political, but they were full of wounds, bruises, and putrifying sores. The faithful city had become a harlot. They offered sacrifice to God with hands full of blood and sin and hearts full of pride. Prophet and priest were all corrupt. Children behaved wickedly against old people; mothers taught their daughters evil ways, and fathers their sons. Oppression reigned on every side.

At such times the righteous almost faint in heart. They wonder what is the hope of the land. At this time God showed the groaning heart of Isaiah the deliverance He was going to give His people from the power of sin. He showed him a man coming meek, lowly, unpretentious, and marred in vision [*sic* visage; see Isaiah 52:14, KJV], and God took this man and laid the sins of the people on Him and put Him to death for them. Is not that marvelous? "The Lord hath laid on Him the iniquity of us all."

I. Behold the great love of God displayed toward us in the text, in that it pleased Him to bruise Christ on our behalf.

II. Behold what the Christ as our sin offering procures for us.

III. Behold also what is required of us in order to enjoy freedom from sin. On these three points we shall now speak, with the Lord helping in the Spirit.

Although Jones might have gleaned these insights from the biblical text itself, it is also likely that they reflect his higher education.

By saying that love is God's motivation, Jones brings a very Christian, New Testament interpretation to the Isaiah passage.

I. Behold the great love of God displayed toward us in that it pleased Him to bruise Christ on our behalf. This love is the fountain of our salvation; a deep, eternal love it is which never fails. When we know and believe the love that God has [for] us, it inspires us to love Him and encourages us to follow Him in a walk of love.

Love for the world prompted God to do this. God so loved the world that He gave His only begotten Son that whosoever believeth in Him should not perish but have everlasting life [John 3:16].

Jeremiah 31[:3] says, "I have loved thee with an everlasting love; therefore with lovingkindness have I drawn thee." In the deep, fathomless heart of divine love, as immeasurable as infinite immensity, yet as wise and holy and just as God can be, God foreknew our sins and, laying them all on Jesus, put them away from us.

Our consolation is that this is God's own plan, His own scheme of love whereby He outwits the powers of hell and delivers the objects of His tender affection. God laid our sins on Jesus. We did not know how to do it. God fixed it for us so we would be bothered about nothing. All we have to do is to believe the testimony and set to our seal that God is true. To us there is no sin — none. God did away with it in Jesus Christ. Divine love, disinterested love, which cannot be understood till believed, did away with our sins by finding for us a substitute, a sin-offering. How we insult and grieve that love when we refuse to accept Jesus.

II. Let us notice what Christ as our sin offering procures for us. "He shall see His seed." The result of the atonement made for us in Christ and our acceptance thereof is that we become children of God, the seed of Christ. To redeem us, He was deprived of earthly Fatherhood; there was no one to declare His generation; like the eunuch, he was a dry tree; yet in the house of His Father He got a name better than of sons and daughters after a fleshly sense. He got a seed that should serve Him to all generations [Ps. 22]. He is elected to a higher fatherhood than Adam or Abraham or David and instead of His fathers they become His sons [Ps. 45]. We become children of God by faith in Christ Jesus, and if children, then heirs, heirs of God and joint heirs with Christ [Rom. 8:17]. Heirs of the fullness and power of the Holy Spirit; heirs to daily grace and access to God; heirs to all the world; and heirs to all the peace, honor, and felicity of glory eternal.

"Therefore let no man glory in men: for all things are yours;

Whether Paul, or Apollos, or Cephas, or the world, or life, or death, or things present, or things to come; all are yours;

And ye are Christ's; and Christ is God's" [1 Cor. 3:21-23].

Are not these things worth having? I, for one, esteem them so. I would rather miss all else than the glory of salvation in Christ. If I must lose friends, the kindness and love of relatives, the esteem of my brethren in church or ministry, my home and shelter, even all that men covet or hold dear, let it be so, and let me be happy with Jesus alone.

God hath procured for me, in the predetermined death of His Son, both justification of life and sanctification of disposition, both the forgiveness of sins and the cleansing of my nature. Jesus to sanctify me with His own blood suffered without the gate [Heb. 13:12]. Let me enjoy this, for all else is trash and vanity. My sins and my very sin[ful] nature were laid on Jesus, that I might be made free from sin, its defilement, its death-dealing power, and its awful penalties of disease, shame, and dishonor, and become a servant to God. Shall I stubbornly and in unbelief defeat the ends of grace and become a castaway from my eternal, blood-bought privileges? God forbid. God grant both you and me to be wiser than that. Eternity will reveal to us what it means to know God in Christ.

III. Behold also what is required of us in order to enjoy personally the benefits procured for us in Christ. "When thou shalt make His soul an offering for sin." Soul means life. The life is in the blood. God provided the life, the blood of Christ as my propitiation for sin, that through the same my sin might be covered, carried away, blotted out, pardoned, and remembered no more; that through the pouring out of His life unto death I might enter into life. God laid my sin on Christ, and the enemy punished sin to utmost satisfaction. But the benefit of the atonement or satisfaction rendered [is] mine only as I agree with what God has done. I must see my lost condition and abhor myself because of the vileness of my nature and the heinousness of my sin. Then I hear the voice of mercy and flee for a refuge to lay hold on the hope set before me. I must accept the sin offering God has given me. I must agree to the divine arrangement whereby God has done away with my sin and rejoice and be glad in it. Hallelujahs of praise will then be mine, for I will be the seed of God, an heir with Jesus Christ His Son.

If God has laid our sin on Jesus, brother, sister, friend, surely it is not on you and me. "All we like sheep have gone astray; we have turned everyone to his own way; and God hath laid on Him the iniquity of us all." That includes you, does it not? Let your heart believe it then, and you are free.

This is the hope of the sinner craving pardon — make His soul your offering for sin. In other words, believe God's testimony concerning His Son:

If we receive the witness of men, the witness of God is greater: for this is the witness of God which He hath testified of His Son.
He that believeth not on the Son of God hath made Him a liar; because he believeth not the record that God gave of His Son.
And this is the record, that God hath given to us eternal life, and this life is in His Son.
He that hath the Son hath life; and he that hath not the Son of God hath not life.

1 John 5:9-12

Believe the record. That is all that is required of you and me — believe the record. Nothing else will save us. Believing in Christ's finished work, in what God has done for us in

A hallmark of Holiness thought, reaching back to its origins in early Wesleyanism, is affirming justification (forgiveness) and sanctification (the breaking of sin's power and the cleansing of human nature) as distinct experiences of salvation. Oftentimes, this sets up a presumption of Christians having two distinct, recognizable experiences.

One can almost hear the invitation of the altar call coming from Jones's insistence that people respond to what God has done. The theological question which Jones leaves unanswered is whether people have the natural ability to "agree with what God has done" and "see [their] lost condition" or whether those capacities have to be granted by God himself.

One wonders if Jones is establishing a position in the finished work controversy that arose in Pentecostalism starting in 1910. Unlike the earlier Wesleyan position that saw sanctification as a distinct experience subsequent to initial salvation/justification/new birth, finished work advocates stressed that the believer need only appropriate the benefits of Christ's finished work on Calvary. The result was an approach to holiness that made it less distinctly a single experience and more progressive.

Jones appears to be saying that the Holy Spirit witnesses to the experience of sanctification which was provided by Christ's death.

Christ, we are forgiven. And if we want purity of heart or sanctification of life that cometh from the same source, we believe the record, and the thing is done. It was all finished at Calvary, and believing we have it. Faith is the substance of things hoped for. If you have the faith, you have the things, because God has ordained it so.

Be like Mr. Duncan. We said, "If God said it is so, it must be so. Don't you see it just could not be otherwise, because God could not lie." We were quoting 1 John 5:1: "Whosoever believeth that Jesus is the Christ is born of God." Directly the light flashed in. He saw that God was true and every man a liar. He rose with a shout of joy and said, "Yes, I see, I see." The word of God in that moment had become real truth to him and so saved him. Jesus has finished the work. You make Jesus your sin offering by believing that your sins were taken off you by a loving heavenly Father and laid on Him. Say, "Amen. God said it, and they are there, on Him, not on me. I believe; I am saved. I have God's unfailing word." Believe it and live.

And as I said, you who want sanctification should remember that He hath made Him to be sin for us who knew no sin, that we might be made the righteousness of God in Him [2 Cor. 5:21].

"For by one offering He hath perfected forever them that are sanctified.

Whereof the Holy Ghost also is a witness to us" [Heb. 10:14-15].

It is all given us right at Calvary[,] where of the upper room, the Holy Ghost given, is a witness unto us. All blessings come upon our faith in what was done on Calvary. Trust the atonement. Rest wholly, everybody, on the finished work of Christ. And all hell cannot take your joy, and heaven will be glad over you [Zeph. 3:11-20].

Source: Charles P. Jones, *Sermons of Life and Power* (Jackson, Miss.: Truth Publishing Co., 1913; reprint edition, National Publishing Board, Church of Christ [Holiness] U.S.A., 2004), pp. 5-11.

C. P. Jones's Sermon on the Resurrection

C. P. Jones's Holiness doctrine also shines through this sermon on Christ's resurrection, especially in the section where he proclaims freedom from sin. This section has the categories and favorite biblical texts of the Holiness movement. The sermon is remarkable for how it first describes the resurrection as God's saving activity played out on a cosmic backdrop ("God brought back the human race from Hades . . ."), not simply as an isolated historical event or even as an event with a primary meaning limited to individual benefit.

RISEN WITH CHRIST

"If ye then be risen with Christ, seek those things which are above, where Christ sitteth on the right hand of God.

Set your affection on things above, not on things on the earth.

For ye are dead, and your life is hid with Christ in God.

When Christ, who is our life, shall appear, then shall ye also appear with Him in glory."

Col. 3:1-4

The great fact that brought hope back to the hearts of Jesus' disciples whence it had fled during the darkness that attended his awful crucifixion was that He verily rose from the dead and showed Himself to them by infallible signs and proofs. The fact of Christ's resurrection the Jews sought hard to suppress. They bribed the guard of His tomb to say that His disciples came and stole His body away while they slept, and this the men did despite the miracle that was wrought before their eyes. Yet the truth came out, as it always will.

Next the rulers of the Jews forbade the gospel ministers to preach that Christ rose, but they proclaimed it all the more. Paul did not believe it, but Jesus appeared to him on the way to Damascus and convinced him. The Greeks derided such a doctrine as inconsistent with all scientific fact and deduction, as a mere matter of harebrained foolishness.

And why such opposition to a great fact attested and witnessed to by God, angels, and men? Ah, at the back of it all was Satan — Satan, who wanted to hold Jesus in the grave, but could not. The resurrection of Jesus stood for so much. It stood for His own victory, and for the victory of all who believe in Him over every aim, plan, and effort of Satan and all his artful hosts combined. In this text we are concerned with two things especially, and maybe three or four:

I.   The fact of Christ's resurrection;

II.   Our resurrection with Christ;

III.   The blessings conferred on us thereby; and

IV.   The splendid hope that this resurrection gives us.

I. The fact of Christ's resurrection. It is important that this fact be established in our minds, for the scriptures say, "If thou shalt confess with thy mouth the Lord Jesus and shalt believe in thine heart that God hath raised Him from the dead, thou shalt be saved" [Rom. 10:9, KJV]. Paul declared (in First Corinthians 15) that if Christ be not raised, our faith is vain, and we are yet in our sins. The hope He always held out to His disciples as He journeyed on to the cross and to the grave was that He would rise again the third day.

So it is not only as an historical fact that we view Christ's resurrection, it is as the foundation of saving faith. It is the basic doctrine of all our hopes. If Christ be not risen, our faith is vain; we are yet in our sins. So faith alone does not save. It depends on whether or not falsehood or eternal truth is back of faith.

We rejoice in the clearly proven fact of the Savior's resurrection, and that not only have we the testimony of men to that fact but the testimony of the Holy Ghost as well.

But as I said, there is more connected with the resurrection of Jesus than merely the physical fact — it stands for all that pertains to human salvation. When God raised Christ from the dead, He brought back the human race from Hades, so to speak, and banished the power of death and took the victory from the grave. The birth of Jesus without His death and resurrection would have meant to the world only what the birth of Moses meant to the Jews, Zoroaster to the Persians, Confucius to the Chinese, Socrates and Plato to the Greeks, and the like. He would merely have been a philosopher and teacher who would have reformed men without saving them, instructed them without delivering them, giving them manners without giving them character, and yet leaving an aching void in their hearts.

II. Let us attend then, secondly in our argument, to the thought of our resurrection with Christ. If this text infers irrefutably that Christ rose, it also infers that we rose with Him. We? Who? Why, all men and especially those who believe He died for all. He rose for all. All were in Him when He died; all were in Him when He rose. But only those who by the Spirit believe this truth (and one cannot believe it but by the Spirit), get the eternal benefit thereof. All get a certain temporal benefit, for it is written that he is the Savior of all men, especially of those who believe [1 Tim. 4:10]. Moses in Arabia could not rule Israel in Egypt. He had to come get them and take them out. Joshua in Canaan could not bless Israel in the desert. He had to suffer with them till in and with him they passed over and were all together. So a risen Savior rules a risen people.

All who serve Christ are with Him. [They are] with Him in sentiment, in doctrine, in faith, in hope, in aim, in effort. They have necessarily died to their own thoughts, to their own wills, to their own carnal hopes, to their own rules and laws, their own associates, and methods and plans, and have taken His.

Deeper than that: we are with Him in the mighty, all-comprehensible, undefeatable purposes of God. God saw us in Him in eternity, and the works were finished before the foundation of the world. So then in the eternal purposes of God these things were true and in due

Notice the cosmic interpretation of the effects of Christ's resurrection. God is working out salvation on a broad level as well as an individual level.

These references, along with vocabulary choices throughout his writing, suggest that Jones was anticipating a significant level of education among either his listeners or his readers.

Again, Jones does not see God's saving activity in Christ — or even our participation in it — as simply an isolated historical event.

time became actual facts — we were born again in Him, in Him we magnified the law, in Him we paid the penalty of sin, and in Him we rose to a new life. Risen with Christ. With Him in His life, the believer is also with Him in His death and with Him in His resurrection and with Him in His fight against sin.

When the apostle uttered the text, He had in mind what he had said a few moments before:

Buried with him in baptism, wherein also ye are risen with him through the faith of the operation of God, who hath raised him from the dead. And you, being dead in your sins and the uncircumcision of your flesh, hath he quickened together with him, having forgiven you all trespasses; blotting out the handwriting of ordinances that was against us, which was contrary to us, and took it out of the way, nailing it to his cross; and having spoiled principalities and powers, he made a shew of them openly, triumphing over them in it. Col. 2:12-15.

Let it be noted that though we all died and arose with Christ, as we were all created in Adam, yet we do not get the spiritual and eternal benefit thereof till we believe in Him. Therefore he that believeth and is baptized shall be saved, and he that believeth not shall be damned [Mark 16:14-16].

III. Let us now notice the blessings conferred on us by our resurrection with Christ.

1. Freedom from sin. The cross of Jesus was the death of sin; therefore the sanctification of every believer and of all the church, which is Christ's body, was accomplished when Jesus died. "It is finished" meant more than many people suppose. If it had not, the gospel would never have been good news, glad tidings, message joyful, "good spell." Calvary meant holiness as well as redemption. For that reason every believer is a saint, though without holiness no man can see the Lord [Hebrews 12:14], yet so great was the sanctifying power of Calvary that the thief could immediately go with Jesus into Paradise, though Pentecost had not yet come. To Pentecost belong the empowering, the witnessing, and the renewing, but to Calvary belong the redeeming, the saving, the sanctifying. To satisfy your mind on this matter, please read Hebrews 1:1-3 and 9:13-14; 10:1-4; and 13:11-12; with Titus 3:4-7 and references. The doctrine of holiness is not scripturally understood and taught by many dirhstaeents [denominations?; misspelling in original] and earnest, noble advocates. Holiness, complete, saving, unquestionable, . . . unimpeachable, incorruptible, and heaven-endorsed holiness we get on Calvary. We have no right to carry any kind of sin from Calvary into the church or to the upper room, for all sin was done away at Calvary. Praise God. Therefore he that believeth is not confounded. When Paul asks, "Shall we continue in sin, that grace may abound," he answers, "How shall we that are dead to sin live any longer therein?" He refers at once to our death and resurrection with Christ, declaring virtually that our baptism sets forth the great truth that "our old man hath been crucified with Him" and that we "rise to walk in newness

Jones is trying to make the basic point that through Christ God can do more with sin in the human person than just forgive it. At its root and in its origins in Wesleyanism, Holiness doctrine is optimistic about the transformation God can produce in a person.

Hebrews 12:14 had been a favorite proof text of sanctification advocates since 18th-century Methodism. Jones's distinction between Pentecost and Calvary seems to be his way of distinguishing the roles of the Holy Spirit (Pentecost) and Jesus Christ (Calvary) in salvation.

of life." Read Romans, 6th chapter. See what complete divorcement from sin we get there. See that in view of this great fact we are to reckon, esteem, think ourselves dead indeed unto sin, but alive unto God through Jesus Christ — not dead to acts of sin, not dead to the past life, not sin put under and kept down, but "dead indeed unto sin and alive to God [Rom. 6:11]. We are on the God side of the cross, as one puts it. We are on the resurrection side, while sin was fully dealt with and left at the cross. Any victory that sin gains over the believer comes through his ignorance of this great truth: "Ye shall know the truth, and the truth shall make you free" [John 8:30-36].

2. The next blessing we get through the resurrection of Christ and our rising with Him is freedom from the Mosaic law. This is hinted at in the second chapter of Colossians in the verses we have quoted. It is also treated at length in the seventh chapter of Romans. Christ was made under the law. In Him we obeyed the law and paid its penalties, for God "laid on Him the iniquity of us all," and "He bore our sicknesses and carried our sorrows." When He rose, death had no more dominion over Him, neither had the law, neither had sin. For this reason the first day of the week became as holy as any, and it was possible for Paul to speak of days as he did in Romans 14:5 and Galatians 4:9-11 and Colossians 2:15. A new covenant is in force in the power of Christ's resurrection. There is a new priesthood, even a risen priest with the power of an endless life and a new law with a new covenant founded on better promises. The old died on Calvary, and the new there went into force, and in fifty days the Holy Spirit came to attest the great and eternal fact.

Now we are free, as free as God can make us. Law does not frighten us, sin has no dominion over us, death cannot claim us, the grave cannot hold us. We are children of the free woman.

The fourth proposition of our text — for want of time we will have to defer to another discourse. God bless you. Be free, for Christ died to free you. Believe in Him, abide in Him, hope in Him, rejoice in Him. He that believeth on this foundation shall not be confounded. Amen.

Source: Charles P. Jones, *Sermons of Life and Power* (Jackson, Miss.: Truth Publishing Co., 1913; reprint edition, National Publishing Board, Church of Christ [Holiness] U.S.A., 2004), pp. 54-60.

By describing Christians as "children of the free woman," Jones is using Galatians 4 to make the point that faith in Christ opens up the saving promises of God.

His acknowledgment of having to quit because of lack of time is a good sign that the sermon was actually preached and bears some of the oral qualities of his preaching.

Theology of Worship Documents

*C. P. Jones's Increasing Discomfort with Denominations
and Denominational Names*

*Included in the depositions of testimony taken in the lawsuit between the warring factions of
Mt. Helm Baptist Church in the late 1890s was a letter written by C. P. Jones to a state denominational official of the Missionary Baptist Church in Mississippi. Responding to the official's
insinuation that he is not truly Baptist, Jones lays out his arguments for why it is unscriptural
to be called "Baptist" and, by implication, why it is unscriptural for the official to desire to be
identified as "Baptist." Jones's 1898 letter, written the same month as the State Baptist Association disassociated itself from him, accentuates the issue of what it means for a church to consider
itself scriptural, an issue at the heart of his ruptures with Mississippi Baptists and later with
Charles Mason and emergent Pentecostalism. His emphasis on recovering the New Testament
church has been a recurring desire among Protestants, as has (among some) the willingness to
use only New Testament appellations.*

"We are Baptists," you say, "because we believe in baptism by immersion and dip because we
fulfill in so doing all righteousness."[31]

My dear brother, you talk strangely. Surely you did not think of what you said. Christ was
dipped to fulfill all righteousness. Did he call himself after John the Baptist; did he say that
the last in the Kingdom of Heaven should be greater than John?[32] Was the church at Jerusalem called a "Baptist Church" or the one at Antioch or any of the earlier churches? Were they
not simply called churches, "the church of God" at such a place, the churches of God, the
churches of the Lord, etc.?

How long has there been a Baptist denomination existing? Was no one immersed up to
the time of Christ, up to three hundred and seventy-five years ago? If the Baptist churches
now called form a denomination, and the denomination be identified with the name Baptist,
it has very little advantage on the Methodist or the Episcopalian denominations. It has not
existed long. It cannot claim apostolic succession.

Denominationalism is unscriptural. Read First Corinthians, [the] first, second, and
third chapters prayerfully and closely. Note in the first chapter, verses ten to sixteen, [and]
in the third chapter, verses three to eight. Again, your statement will not hold good [i.e., will
not hold up], but the so-called Campbellites, who refused to call themselves anything but

> Jones first repeats
> the standard Baptist
> apology for why the
> name is a good one.
> He counters by argu-
> ing that Christ was
> immersed and did not
> call himself a Baptist.
> Likewise, none of the
> early churches were
> called Baptist.

> Jones contradicts a
> popular Baptist idea,
> particularly among
> Landmark Baptists,
> that their church can
> be directly traced back
> to the first century.

31. Compare Matthew 3:15.
32. See Matthew 11:11.

Christians, and the Seventh Day Adventists, who accepted a denominational name outside of God, [and] the Greek church, [which is] an established state institution, and the Dunkard and other denominations all dip, but they are not called Baptists on account thereof.[33] That theory therefore does not hold.

I have carefully reasoned and prayed over these things and have not dared move till the Holy Spirit moved me. Besides, my brother, you seemed to have overlooked the plain statement of the Scripture that the whole family in heaven and earth should be named after the Father of our Lord Jesus Christ — Eph. 3:14. And [thus] you are now fighting against the name of God in favor of a three hundred and seventy-five year old tradition. . . .

. . . Away with man's tradition, and give us the word of God. The Baptists claim to be right and everybody else wrong, yet they fellowship [with] the most ungodly men, setting them up as teachers and leaders, [and] set[ting] up their work in an unscriptural [way] and contend[ing] for it. They rob Christ. The doctrine of the New Testament is called by them "Baptist Doctrine." [But] the Holy Spirit called it the doctrine of God our Savior. . . . But when a man cares more for the fellowship of men who are called by a certain name than he does for the honor of Jesus Christ, when they seek to yoke that certain name on people rather than the name of Christ, when it means to twist the word of God to suit a certain creed and to work by the added traditions of certain men, when it means for a certain sect of men to dictate what sort of interpretation you put on the word of God and to outlaw you if you believe and practice the word of God just as it is laid down, when it means to fellowship [with] iniquity in high places and fall down at the feet of drunkards and murderers and adulterers and to cover up all manner of sin, when it means to put Bible reading out lest the people get sanctified through the truth — the same thing [for which] Christ died that they might be, namely, sanctified, Eph. 5:25-27; Heb. 13:12 — when it means to fellowship in Convention and Association and Synods [with] Churches that verily hate the word of God, [then] sectarianism is wrong.

If it means to have Christ alone to follow as master, Christ alone to feel bound by his word alone, to love alone what he loves, to hate what he hates, to support what he supports with a free conscience — in short, if it means to make Christ all and in all, [and my] self nothing and men nothing — Eph. 1:21-23; Col. 3:11 — then I am a sectarian with a vengeance. I am as I understand myself to be at first a believer in the Bible only and that the Holy Spirit leads a man into the understanding thereof. . . .

. . . I beg to say that I am not led to dissent from the churches of Christ that are thus walking [i.e., according to apostolic "form, practice, and spirit"][34] but from corrupt and

This emphasis on "Christ alone" anticipates a common emphasis in his songwriting and, indeed, the title to his first published collection the following year: *Jesus Only.*

33. Because there are other churches, by other names, which baptize by immersion, Jones argues that it is illogical for Baptists to appropriate that name because they happen to baptize by immersion, too. "Campbellites" refers to churches historically descended from the Restoration Movement, a religious reform movement from the early nineteenth century in the United States.

34. Ironically, this question of apostolic "form, practice, and spirit" was likely part of the later disagreement between Jones and Charles Mason, after the latter had adopted Pentecostal sensibilities. Early Pentecostals were confident that they had indeed found again apostolic Christianity as compared to other churches. Thus

unscriptural denominationalism, from unscriptural names and methods, from man-made constitutions and institutions, and [to return] to New Testament names and the leadership of the Spirit of God.

Source: C. P. Jones to C. T. Stamps, 20 July 1898, filed as exhibit no. 2 to the C. T. Stamps deposition, *Mt. Helm Baptist Church et al. vs. C. P. Jones et al.,* Box 13903, Series 6, Case 10041, Mississippi Department of Archives and History, pp. 56-57.

Jones would have ended up on the receiving end of the complaint that he and his church were not sufficiently apostolic.

C. P. Jones's Teaching about Worship

The following excerpts come from an early twentieth-century treatise by C. P. Jones to clarify his church's position on key issues. The excerpts selected represent not only entries directly address-ing worship concerns but also categories like his doctrines of the church and of salvation, which often affect how worship is done. The document reflects both Jones's Baptist background (e.g., his use of the word "ordinance" rather than "sacrament" and his rejection of infant baptism) and his position as a Holiness movement minister wanting to draw distinctions between Holiness belief and Pentecostalism. (For example, the defining of the right experiential aspects of sanctification and perfection reflect his Holiness commitments, and rightly explaining "baptism of the Holy Ghost" and bodily healing show his rejection of some forms of Pentecostalism.) The implicit rejec-tion of tongues as the key indicator of being filled with the Spirit suggests that this document was written after 1906.

WHAT WE BELIEVE AND TEACH

We feel as led by the Spirit of God that the time has come for us to set forth in writing those things which we believe and teach, and contend for concerning Jesus Christ and His gospel, as distinguishing us from other professing Christians (Jude 3). Still we believe that there is little on which evangelical Christians do not agree when they understand themselves and one another (1 Corinthians 1:30; Psalm 133; Ephesians 4:1-17), though there are differences of administration, diversities of operations, helps, and governments, even in the Holy Spirit of Christ. We believe that sectarianism is or comes not so much by uniformity of method and organization as by the knowledge of the personal Christ and spirit of love. We gladly set be-fore all, what we believe, teach, and contend for, that they who may be led of the spirit of God in Christ to labor with us may know precisely what to answer those who ask them a reason for their hope with meekness and fear (1 Peter 3:15). We feel it our duty to write the vision and make it plain, that he may run that readeth it (Habakkuk 2:2).

V. Concerning the Church

Concerning the Church we teach, hold, and contend:

1   That the body of the believers in Christ in any one place is the church in that place: that the term "church" means a selected congregation, enjoying certain citizen rights together; that therefore a region [such] as Galatia or Judea may have many churches. But we contend that on account of the unity of Christ, though there be several meetingplaces, there can be but one church in any particular locality. Christ is not sectarian (Revelation 1:1-3; Galatians 1:22; 1 Corinthians 16:19). This does not preclude diversities of opera-

tions, but there must be but one Lord, and He has one body and is not divided. All else is sectarianism and belongs to the flesh.

2   That the church being the body of Christ has as its mission the doing of the will of God in the earth through the indwelling of Christ. To this end she must keep His commandments, observe His ordinance, [and] discipline her members in His word, that this may be done rightly and effectual[ly].

VI. Concerning the Gifts of the Holy Spirit

We believe, hold, teach, contend:

1   That every obedient believer is heir to the gift of the Holy Ghost (Ezekiel 36:27; John 14:17; Galatians 4:6-7).

2   That He is the gift of God in Christ to His people whereby they receive sanctifying, illumination, and witnessing power to obey God's word. He becomes as the sanctifying presence of Christ as He is submitted to the leader and spiritual teacher in the breast of every believer who receives Him (John 14:26; Romans 8:9; 1 Corinthians 3:16; Acts 1:8; 1 John 2:27; John 16:13).

3   That receiving the Holy Ghost is not that same experience as conversion, but is and must be subsequent. One must be converted before he can receive the Spirit (Acts 8:14-17; 19:1-4).[35]

4   That the baptism of the Spirit is a term applied to the first outpouring of the Holy Ghost when the whole church was baptized in the one body of Christ, just as the whole church was ransomed in Christ when He died. That always after Pentecost and the conversion of Cornelius the Holy Spirit is referred to as a gift (Acts 2:38-39), a receiving (Acts 19:1-2), a filling (Ephesians 5:6-18), an anointing (1 John 2:27; 1 Corinthians 1:21). Especially is the term "anointing" applied to the gift of the Holy Ghost in the life of Christ (Acts 10:38; Isaiah 61:1-3; Hebrews 1:9; Luke 4:18).

VII. Concerning Regeneration

We believe, teach, and contend that to enter the kingdom of heaven a man must be born from above (John 3:1-16):

1   That the new birth is spiritual and divine, that which is born of flesh being flesh and that which is born of the spirit being spirit.

2   That the spiritual nature so born is divine (1 Peter 1:4) and cannot sin (1 John 3:9-10).

35. The influence of the Holiness movement on Jones's thinking is evident in two respects in this discussion of the Holy Spirit. One is in connecting the Spirit to sanctification, the other in assuming that there is a second distinct experience that comes after initial conversion or salvation. For Jones, speaking in tongues is not evidence of the Spirit's infilling.

3   That sin can only come from the fleshly mind, which if we live after we shall die (Romans 8:1-13; 8:16-23; Galatians 6:7-8).

4   That in the new birth we are begotten by the word of truth in the will of God (John 1:11-13; James 1:16-18).

5   That regeneration, being an act of faith, imparts a cleansing to the whole being, morally speaking, even to body, soul, and spirit (Titus 3:5; Acts 15:7-11). That it embraces repentance toward God and faith toward our Lord Jesus Christ (Acts 20:21).

VIII. Concerning Church Ordinances

We believe, teach, and contend:

1   That Jesus ordered that they who believe in His name be baptized into the name of the Lord Jesus Christ or of the Father, Son, and Holy Ghost (Matthew 28:19-20; Mark 16:14-16; Acts 19:1-5; Acts 10:44-48).

2   That baptism is the burial in water and rising (Romans 6:1-7) setting forth the death and resurrection of Christ and our death and resurrection in Him (Galatians 2:20-21; 3:26-27).

3   That baptism belongs to the believer in the gospel as the first required act of obedience: then Jesus blessed infants but did not baptize them, nor did his disciples.

4   That the Lord's Supper was instituted when our Lord celebrated His last Passover with His disciples and is to be celebrated as often as we do it to show forth the Lord's death till He comes again (Matthew 26:26-29; Mark 14:22-25; Luke 22:19-20).

5   That the Lord's Supper consists of bread and wine for all, typifying the Lord's body broken and His blood shed for all (1 Corinthians 11).

6   That they who partake of the Lord's Supper should discern the Lord's body, that is, its spiritual unity.

7   We practice the washing of feet as obeying the Lord, not as a regular observed ordinance of the Church (John 13:1-7; 1 Timothy 5:9-10).

IX. Concerning Justification

We believe, teach, and contend:

1   That it is the act of grace by which God saves the sinners on the merits of Jesus Christ; God having so dealt with the sinner and with sin in the death and resurrection of Jesus Christ, as the propitiation for the sins, that He may be just and yet justify the ungodly (Romans 3:24; 4:24; 5:1-21).

2   That justification is wholly by grace on the merits of Christ and not by works of the law. It is the act of grace by which [God] declares men righteous (Romans 3:20; Galatians 2:16-21).

Jones, likely reflecting his Baptist background, uses the terminology of ordinance, rather than sacrament, in speaking of baptism and the Lord's Supper. This way of speaking is often a sign that a person will more strongly emphasize human activity than divine in these two rites, as Jones does here.

The word "ordinance" is related to the idea that Jesus ordered or commanded these practices. Accordingly, they are viewed as important times of obedience to the express command of Christ. The inclusion of foot-washing follows from this same premise, since Jesus commanded it, too.

3   That when a sinner believes in Jesus the merit of Christ's perfect righteousness is imputed to him (Romans 4), [the] Son justifying him in God's sight (Romans 5:1).[36]

4   That justification includes the benefits of pardon and, in a sense, of holiness and all the riches of grace, since it declares us righteous and makes us new.

5   Adoption is that aspect of justification by which faith in Christ makes us children of God and heirs of His promises (Galatians 3:22-29).

X. Concerning Sanctification

We believe, teach, and contend:

1   That the believer is called unto holiness (1 Thessalonians 4:3-8; Luke 1:73-75).

2   That we are to be holy in all manner of conversation, which means all phases of life (1 Peter 1:13-16; 2 Peter 3:13-18; 1 John 3:7).

3   That without holiness we cannot see God (Hebrews 12:1-14; Matthew 7:21-28).[37]

4   That holiness is essential to acceptable service with God (2 Timothy 2:21; Hebrews 12:28-29).

5   That Jesus sanctified all believers in the will of God when He died (Hebrews 10:10-12). Therefore in God's sight all believers are saints incorporated by faith into the one holy body of Christ.

6   That we are to make this work of the cross and of Jesus' blood (Hebrews 1:1-3; 9:12-14; 10:24-31; 13:12-21) practical and true in our lives by faith (Acts 15:6-9; 9:34; 16:18) and obedience.

7   That the Holy Spirit applies the blood of Jesus for our sanctification as we believe for the same [as we believe God will sanctify] (Mark 9:23-24; 11:22-24; 2 Thessalonians 2:13; 1 John 5:4).

8   That the word of God is as the blood of Jesus [so] that in the hands of the Holy Spirit our sanctification is effected (John 17:17; Ephesians 5:25-27). Therefore it is essential to the continued sanctification of believers that they assemble themselves together and be fed on the word of God (Hebrews 10:24-39; John 21:15-17; 8:30-35; Ephesians 4:1-16; Proverbs 21:1-22; Psalms 19:7-14; 119:11).

9   That the Bible does not say "get sanctified" but "be ye holy," showing that every arrangement is made and that so [as] soon as we put our lives on the altar (Christ), the altar sanctifies the gift (Matthew 23:19).

---

36. In justification God imputes righteousness to us (God counts us righteous through faith in Christ), whereas in sanctification God imparts righteousness to us (God inwardly transforms us into being more righteous through Jesus Christ). The distinction was found in the Holiness movement because of the popularizing of the notion of sanctification by John Wesley, founder of Methodism in the 18th century.

37. This proof text from Hebrews was been one of the most important ones among sanctification advocates since 18th-century Methodism. It was used to emphasize the necessity of an experience of sanctification.

10 That Christ is holiness to all who obey and abide in Him, and there is no real holiness apart from Him (1 Corinthians 1:30-31; John 15:1-10; Galatians 3:1-4; John 14:6).

11 That experimental holiness includes separation [from evil] unto God (2 Corinthians 6:14-20; 7:1; Hebrews 12:1, 14; 2 Timothy 2:20, 22), devotion to God in Christ and to His will (Romans 12:1-2; 1 Thessalonians 4:3, 7), and moral cleanliness (Exodus 13:2; Genesis 2:3; 19:10, 14, 23-24; Joshua 7:13).

12 That the duty of every believer is to instantly seek holiness till he finds that the Holy Spirit of Jesus by the blood has brought every part of his being into the will of God. Then go on to perfection in the grace of holiness, being by the spirit renewed day by day (Titus 3:4-5).

"Experimental" is used to mean "experiential" or "experienced."

XI. Concerning Perfection

We believe and teach:

1 That we are to let our hearts be perfect with the Lord our God (Matthew 5:48; 2 Corinthians 13:11; Genesis 17:1; 2 Samuel 22:31).

2 That, experimentally speaking, perfection is of two kinds, present and ultimate. Present perfection refers to the thoroughness with which the blood of Jesus deals with sin of the heart, so that the eye is single and the whole body is full of light. The terms mean wholeheartedness toward God, the opposite of double-mindedness. The man who is so perfected by the blood of Christ is to be marked, and his end is peace (Psalm 37:37). . . . such a one may make mistakes and stumble if unwatchful (1 Kings 15:1-4 with 2 Chronicles 16:7-12), but [he] will not willfully sin against God, because such sin must come out of the heart. Ultimate perfection is that reached through growing in grace and knowledge by suffering with Jesus and seeking and doing the will of God (Hebrews 5:7-9; 1 Peter 4:1-5; 5:10; Philippians 3:15-17).

3 We believe and teach that the scriptures are given to make the men of God perfect from self will, sin, weakness, doubts, fears, [and] ignorances. That to be and keep perfect, the scriptures must be used for teaching, reproof, correction, [and] instruction in righteousness (2 Timothy 3:15-17).

Jones likewise derives the language of "perfection" from the sanctification teachings of John Wesley and the Holiness movement. Here it does not mean a complete absence of flaw or error but the thoroughness by which God can transform the human person. The teaching is an optimistic view that God can do more with sin in a person than just forgive it.

XII. Concerning Temptation

We believe, teach, and contend:

1 That temptation comes to all, but that temptation is not sin (Matthew 4:11; 1 Peter 4:12-14; Hebrews 2:18; James 1:1-5).

2 That God is faithful and will not suffer us to be tempted above that we are able, but will with every temptation make a way of escape, that we may bear it (1 Corinthians 10:13).

The absence of being tempted is not a mark of having experienced sanctification or Christian perfection. Even sanctified Christians can be tempted.

3   That we are to watch and pray against temptation rather than to boast of our own power to overcome (Matthew 6:13; Luke 8:13; 22:40-46).

XIII. Concerning Bodily Healing

We believe, teach, and contend:

1   That physicians and medicines are not denounced in the Bible but are approved for those who desire them (Proverbs 17:22; Ezekiel 47:12; Colossians 4:14; Job 13:4; Jeremiah 8:22; Matthew 9:12; Luke 4:23).

2   But that the Holy Spirit, through the atonement made by Christ, has set gifts of healing in the Church (1 Corinthians 12:4-11; James 5:13-16; 1 Peter 2:24; 3:13; with Deuteronomy 28).

> This passage sets the theological base for Jones's view of how physical healing is possible. Christ's atoning death provides the source, and the Holy Spirit makes this source effective within the church.

3   That Christ is therefore the scripturally recognized healer of His people (Galatians 3:20; 1 Corinthians 1:20-24; Isaiah 33:24; 61:1-3; Psalm 103; 107:1-22). This is [to] the end that affliction may try and increase our faith, and make our communion with God closer and our holiness more perfect (Hebrews 12:5-10), while if we turn to man for deliverance, we lose the spiritual blessing that comes from being delivered by a jealous God (Jeremiah 17:5-9; Psalm 60:11- 12).

4   That in healing His people the Savior in the Holy Spirit uses (a) the prayer of faith with anointing oil (Mark 6:13; James 5:14-16); (b) the prayer of faith alone (Mark 9:21-24; Luke 11:9-14); (c) prayer and fasting and power (Mark 9:27-29; Psalm 35:13; 69:10; 109:24); (d) the word of faith (John 4:46-53; Acts 14:8-10; Matthew 8:5-13); (e) the touch of faith (Matthew 9:20-22; 14:35-36); (f) laying on of hands (Mark 16:18; 1:27-42; Acts 28:8); and (g) the handkerchief or anything from the presence of the healer (Acts 19:11-12).

> Although the first-hand accounts of Christ Temple's worship do not describe practices in detail, it isn't hard to imagine from this list how a healing ministry would have operated in its worship.

5   That when it please God, He uses means of another kind to heal, which he will make known to those who seek Him (Isaiah 38:21; 1 Timothy 5:23).

6   That God is jealous that His people do not seek Him instead of the physician (2 Chronicles 16:12; Jeremiah 17:5; Matthew 11:28; Psalm 118).

> While Jones doesn't condemn seeking human help for illnesses, his point is that a sick person's first and ultimate trust must be in the Lord even when visiting a doctor.

7   That to be assured of divine healing requires that we repent of sin (Psalm 103;107) and that we show mercy to the poor and needy (Isaiah 58; Psalm 41; Proverbs 21:13) and that we pay our vows (Psalm 50:14-15), yet healing may be had entirely by faith where the divine purpose is not disciplinary, but to glorify, by God showing forth His power.

8   One is not compelled to adopt divine healing to be a member with us but must admit its possibility (1 Corinthians 10:31; Ephesians 4:1-15; Isaiah 43:9). It is not considered a matter of discipline to have a physician. According to your faith be it unto you.

XIV. Concerning Spiritual Gifts

We believe, teach and contend:

1   That in the 12th, 13th, and 14th chapters of 1 Corinthians, the nature and purpose of spiritual gifts are set forth.

2   That the Holy Spirit gives these gifts to individuals as He wills (Hebrews 2:4).

3   That no one gift is the specific sign or evidence of the Holy Spirit's presence, but that love (1 Corinthians 13) and power (Acts 1:8) are evidence, not even power alone, for that may be of Satan.

The denial that any one gift is the "specific sign or evidence" counters early Pentecostalism's emphasis on speaking in tongues as the distinctive sign of being filled or baptized with the Holy Spirit.

4   That spiritual gifts may be counterfeited, and though of use to edification, they are not to be trusted as evidence (2 Thessalonians 2:7-12; 2 Timothy 3:8).

5   That there are three abiding saving evidences and essentials of true religion: faith, hope, and love (1 Corinthians 13:13).

6   That the gift of prophecy is accounted by the Holy Spirit most desirable of the gifts as being the most benefit in spreading and edifying the Church.

Source: Charles Price Jones, *What We Believe and Teach,* reprint edition (Jackson, Miss.: National Publishing Board, Church of Christ [Holiness] U.S.A., 2000), pp. 1, 5-13.

C. P. Jones on Baptism and the Lord's Supper

This early sermon by C. P. Jones places baptism and the Lord's Supper within a larger framework of church order — i.e., how the church is to be organized. Rather than calling them sacraments, he called them ordinances, a term which Jones likely saw as more biblical (see the opening Scripture quotations below) and which emphasizes Christ's institution (ordering or ordaining) of them and our use of them as acts of obedience. Throughout the sermon, Jones uses a particular approach to Scripture which seeks to substantiate every element by direct scriptural reference. This method includes an interpretation of the original Greek word for baptism to support immersion only.

BAPTISM AND THE LORD'S SUPPER
(THE GOSPEL ORDINANCES)

"Be ye followers of me, even as I also am of Christ.

Now I praise you, brethren, that ye remember me in all things, and keep the ordinances as I delivered them to you." 1 Cor. 11:1-2.

THERE we have three important things: (1) The minister [as] a follower of Christ; (2) the churches [as] followers of the ministers; and (3) the ordinances to be kept as delivered.

Let us meekly and prayerfully consider them, and may the Lord give us understanding in all things. 2 Tim. 2:7.

I. The Minister [as] a Follower of Christ.

Christ is the Shepherd and Bishop of our souls (1 Pet. 2:25); the way, the truth, and the life (John 14:6); the only faithful and true witness (Rev. 3:14); the Head of the church, which is His body (Eph. 1:22-23); the all in all of redemptive effort (Col. 3:11; Eph. 1:23). He is the word of God (John 1:1-12), the Light of the world (John 8:12), the Bread of Life (John 6:47-58), the Fountain of Living Waters (Jer. 2:13; John 7:37-39), the Lord of the kingdom (Rev. 19:16), the Sabbath of His people (Col. 2:16-17; Heb. 4), the Sacrifice of substitution by whom we have atonement (Heb. 2:9; 9:28), the High Priest of our profession and the apostle of God to us (Heb. 3:1). It is His faith that we confess (Gal. 2:20), His love with which we love (2 Cor. 5:16-17), His doctrine we teach (Titus 2:10), His gospel we preach (Rom. 1:16-17), His church He is building (Matt. 16:16-18), and it is He who does the building (Ps. 127; 1 Cor. 3), we as ministers being workers together with Him.

He, Christ, is our church (1 Cor. 12:1-13), our denomination (Acts 4:9-12), our sect (1 Cor. 2:2), our all. It is to be found in Him that we count all else loss (Phil. 3:1-12). How important,

Although it is impossible to know the changes a sermon goes through from being preached and then published, here Jones does not begin his sermons by telling a personal story. In contrast, he begins by speaking directly about biblical truth without "warming up" the congregation. Can this method of preaching still be effective today?

Having become
pastor of one of the
pre-eminent African-
American Baptist
churches around the
age of 30, Jones must
have experienced
these temptations.

then, how indispensably important that the minister be a follower of Him. Are you a minister? Seek nothing but to follow Christ. Are you a professor of Christ? Do you confess and follow His salvation? Pray for your minister, not that he be a great man, or succeed in the world, but that he follow Christ. It is easy for ministers to go off after great men, lodges, conventions, society, orders, great human endeavors, honors, money, etc. All these seek to lead the minister from Jesus Christ, the real life and way, the real light of the world. It takes prayer to hold him in the narrow path where he knows nothing among men save Jesus Christ and Him crucified. If he lead after any other than the humble, obedient Jesus of the New Testament, he is no safe leader. He will lead you into the pit of hell. The apostolic ministry had no time for these worldly entanglements and testified against them.

Hear Paul:

"No man that warreth entangleth himself with the affairs of this life; that he may please Him who hath chosen him to be a soldier." 2 Tim. 2:4.

Then hear Jesus:

"How can ye believe, which receive honor one of another, and seek not the honor that cometh from God only?" John 5:44.

"And then went great multitudes with Him: and He turned, and said unto them,

'If any man come to Me, and hate not his father and mother, and wife and children, and brethren, and sisters, yea, and his own life also, he cannot be My disciple.' " Luke 14:25-26.

This is the first thing in church order — a Christ-filled and Christ-following ministry.

II. The Next Thing in Church Order Is That the Churches Are to Follow the Ministry.

The church is not a conglomeration of wild-spirited religious people, every man following his own mind and imagination. On the contrary, there is a strongly recognized order, and an established ministry to whom obedience is commanded. This ministry is mentioned in Ephesians 4:10-12.

Ministerial authority is clearly recognized. Christ in Revelation, second and third chapters, did not address the churches directly even through the apostle John, but addressed the angel or messenger or bishop of the church. Paul going up to Jerusalem did the same thing. Acts 15 and Gal. 2.

Now hear the Holy Spirit. Turn first to 1 Thess. 5:12-13:

"And we beseech you, brethren, to know them which labor among you, and are over you in the Lord and admonish you;

And to esteem them very highly in love for their work's sake, and be at peace among yourselves."

Then take 1 Tim. 5:17-18:

"Let the elders that rule well be counted worthy of double honor, especially they who labor in the word and doctrine.

For the Scripture saith, Thou shalt not muzzle the ox that treadeth out the corn. And, The laborer is worthy of his reward."

Turn next to Hebrews 13:7:

"Remember them which have the rule over you, who have spoken unto you the word of God: whose faith follow, considering the end of their conversation."

Then take the 17th verse:

"Obey them that have the rule over you, and submit yourselves: for they watch for your souls, as they that must give account, that they may do it with joy, and not with grief: for that is unprofitable for you." Heb. 13:17.

All this clearly establishes that ministerial authority is vested in elders or bishops, whose qualifications are given us in 1 Timothy, 3rd chapter, and Titus, 1st chapter.

What authority has a shepherd over his sheep? What authority had a judge in Israel or a prince over the tribes? A similar authority has the pastor or bishop in the church.

"Take heed therefore unto yourselves, and to all the flock, over the which the Holy Ghost hath made you overseers, to feed the church of God, which He hath purchased with His own blood." Acts 20:28.

How careful, how prayerful, how faithful, how holy must we be, that we may say to the Lord's flock, "Follow me, as I also follow Christ."

The minister is the church's pattern, her teacher, her ruler, judge, and her medium of blessing even in bodily health. Jas. 5:14, 13. When he walks in the Spirit, they who hear him hear God, for God worketh through him.

III. The Next Point in Church Order
Is the Ordinances. Now an Ordinance Is Any Thing
Ordered or Ordained to Be.

Baptism. The first usually recognized ordinance is baptism. In this Jesus set forth the great fundamental doctrines of salvation, to wit, His own death and resurrection on man's behalf and the death and resurrection of all believers in Him. Every thing in the salvation of man depends on the death and resurrection of Jesus.

(1) Justification. He was delivered for our offenses and raised again for our justification. Rom. 4:25-26.

(2) Upon it depends also our sanctification. How is the question answered, Shall we continue in sin that grace may abound? By the word, "God forbid; how shall we who are dead to sin live any longer therein?" We are then declared to be dead to sin with Christ and raised with Him. Rom. 6:1-23.

Jones explains why he doesn't use the language of "sacraments." As occurs here, calling baptism and the Lord's Supper "ordinances" emphasizes the institution by Christ and their use in obedience by Christians. For many, "sacraments" indicates a higher sense of divine activity in the administration of them.

Jones again uses the twofold concept of salvation found in Holiness movement thinking.

(3) Our power to live with Christ in cleanness, godliness, and heavenliness depends on the death and resurrection of Jesus, as we find by reading Col. 2:10-12 and 3:1-5.

(4) Our regeneration[,] in all that term means[,]"depends on the death and resurrection of Jesus"; for we read in 1 Pet. 1:3-4,

"Blessed be the God and Father of our Lord Jesus Christ, which according to His abundant mercy hath begotten us again unto a lively hope by the resurrection of Jesus Christ from the dead,

To an inheritance incorruptible, and undefiled, and that fadeth not away, reserved in heaven for you."

(5) The answer of a good conscience, in this sense saving us.

"The like figure whereunto even baptism doth also now save us (not the putting away of the filth of the flesh, but the answer of a good conscience toward God), by the resurrection of Jesus Christ." 1 Pet. 3:21.

(6) It is also the earnest and herald of our bodily resurrection, in which we hope. We must keep the doctrine of the resurrection in remembrance if we would be saved. 1 Cor. 15:1-4.

It was for this that Peter and Paul and all the early ministry suffered (see 2 Tim. 2:8-10), that we might know the power of the resurrection life.

So important was this truth concerning death and resurrection in the scheme of redemption that it was set before our minds in the ordinance or rite of baptism. Every Christian should be able to think of his baptism and be able to say with Paul,

"I am crucified with Christ: nevertheless I live; yet not I, but Christ liveth in me: and the life which I now live in the flesh I live by the faith of the Son of God, who loved me, and gave Himself for me." Gal. 2:20.

The apostles all followed Christ in the practice of water immersion, for that is what the word *baptidzo* means.

Finding the method of baptism by close definition of this Greek New Testament word has been a common feature of Baptist thought. Most of this sermon would have been the same if Jones had preached it while still pastor of Mt. Helm.

The Lord's Supper. The Lord, on the night of His betrayal, took bread and wine and instituted a feast to commemorate the breaking of His body and the shedding of His blood on our behalf. While the ministers alone at that time partook, still later we see the churched engaged in it. Acts 2:42; 20:11; 1 Cor. 5:7-11. Matthew, Mark, and Luke practically agree in their account of the institution of this supper. It was to show forth Christ's death. It was to look forward to His second coming. It was to be eaten as His body and blood, without which there is no life. May we without cavil in all things follow Him and keep His commandments. O God, forsake us not, but show us how to follow Thee. Incline our hearts to that obedience to thy commandments (Rev. 22:14; 1 John 2:4), that obedience of faith, without which we have no right to the tree of life. Forgive us, cleanse us, heal us, sanctify us, and lead us on to glory. Rom. 8:16-18. Amen.

Source: Charles P. Jones, *Sermons of Life and Power* (Jackson, Miss.: Truth Publishing Co., 1913; reprint edition, National Publishing Board, Church of Christ [Holiness] U.S.A., 2004), pp. 141-47.

Denominational Statements on Worship-related Issues

The short doctrinal statement printed in the denomination's first polity manual in 1926 summarizes Jones's longer statement found above. Note how each article is short except for the lists of points provided to explain the gift of the Holy Spirit, spiritual gifts, and divine healing. These lists likely reflect areas where Jones and denominational officials felt it necessary to distinguish Holiness teachings from Pentecostalism.

VIII. JUSTIFICATION

We believe that justification is God's work done for us, by which full pardon is granted to all who believe and receive Jesus Christ as Savior and Lord. Rom. 3:24; Acts 10:43.

IX. REGENERATION

We believe that regeneration is the new birth, that is, God's work done in us, by which the believer is given a spiritual life, and rectifying the attitude of the will toward God and holy things. John 3:6; 2 Tim. 3:5.

X. SANCTIFICATION

We believe that sanctification is that act of Divine grace whereby we are made Holy. In justification, the guilt of sin is removed; in regeneration, the love of sin is removed; in sanctification, the inclination to sin is removed. Sanctification must be definitely experienced to fit us to see the Lord. 1 Thess. 5:23; Heb. 10:14; John 17:17; Heb. 12:1-14.[38]

XIII. BAPTISM

We believe that baptism is commanded of our Lord and that it belongs to the believer of the gospel, "not infants who cannot believe," and that the Bible [biblical] way of administering it is by immersion. Matt. 28:19-20; Mark 16:14-16; Rom. 6:1-7.

XIV. THE LORD'S SUPPER

We believe that the Lord's Supper is a New Testament Ordinance, and that it was instituted when our Lord celebrated His last Passover with His disciples, and that it consists of

Despite the denomination's having picked up some elements of Methodism, it did not adopt classic Methodism's acceptance of infant baptism and the use of a variety of modes of baptism. Here the church continued to embrace the believer's baptism sentiments it would have had as a Baptist congregation.

---

38. With these affirmations, the denomination is affirming Holiness sentiments that can be traced back to the 18th century and early Methodists who believed that sanctification was a distinct experience.

bread and wine, and that as often as we take it we show forth the Lord's death till He comes again. Matt. 26:26-29; Mark 14:22-25; Luke 22:19-20; 1 Cor. 11:23-24; 1 Cor. 5.

XV. The Gift of the Holy Ghost

(a) We believe that every true believer is heir to the gift of the Holy Ghost. Gal. 4:6-7.

(b) We believe that He is the gift of God in Christ Jesus to the children of God, sanctifying, quickening, guiding into all truth, and giving power to obey and witness [to] God's Word. John 14:16-26; Acts 1:8.

(c) We believe that the receiving of the Holy Ghost is subsequent to conversion. Acts 8:14-16; 19:1-4.

(d) We believe that a backslider must be reclaimed before he or she can receive the Holy Ghost.

(e) We believe that the Holy Ghost baptized the whole church on the day of Pentecost because of the Jewish nation, and the whole church in Cornelius's house because of the gentile nation; and that always thereafter, He is referred to as a gift, Acts 2:38-39; a receiving, Acts 19:1-2; a filling, Eph. 5:18; an anointing, John 2:27; 2 Cor. 1:21. He is never again referred to as a baptism, for there is but one baptism. Eph. 4:1, 5.

These statements on the Holy Spirit are apparently meant to undercut Pentecostal emphases on using key events in Acts to establish a paradigm for ongoing Christian experience.

XVI. Foot-Washing

We believe in foot-washing as an act of obedience in following the example given by our Lord Jesus Christ.

XVII. Spiritual Gifts

We believe that Spiritual Gifts are set forth in the 12th, 13th, and 14th chapters of First Corinthians.

1   That no one gift is the specific (sign) or evidence of the Holy Spirit's presence, but faith (Heb. 11:1) and love (2 Cor. 13) are the evidence; not even power alone is the evidence, for that may be of Satan.

2   That these gifts, though they may be of use to edification, may be counterfeited and are not to be trusted as evidence. 2 Thess. 2:7-12; 2 Tim. 3:8.

3   That there are three essential evidences of true religion: Faith, Hope, and Love. 1 Cor. 13:13.

4   That the Bible endorses speaking in tongues, or a gift of tongues, but that no one really speaks in tongues unless he speaks a language understood by men, as in Acts 2.

Each of these affirmations is intended to undercut a classic Pentecostal emphasis on speaking in tongues as being the necessary, biblical evidence of being filled with the Holy Spirit.

5   That though one speak with tongues, it is no evidence of the Holy Ghost at all, but merely a sign.

XVIII. DIVINE HEALING

1   We do not condemn physicians and medicines because the Bible does not. Prov. 17:22; Ezek. 47:12; Col. 4:14; Matt. 9:12.

2   We believe and teach Divine Healing according to the Scriptures.

3   We believe it is a gift set in the Church and that the prayer of faith will save the sick and the Lord will raise them up. James 5:15.

Like some strands of the Holiness movement (and Pentecostalism), this denomination maintained an emphasis on physical healing.

Source: *Manual of the History, Doctrine, Government, and Ritual of the Church of Christ (Holiness) U.S.A.,* 1st ed. (Norfolk, Va.: Guide Publishing Company, 1926), pp. 14-27.

Polity Documents

Denominational Policies on Church Membership, Ministry, Women, and the Church

The first published organizational manual for the denomination defines policies on several worship-related issues. The policies reflect the mid-1920s, probably a period of stabilizing and maturing for the fledgling denomination, of which Christ Temple was the "mother church." The first excerpts come from the chapter on the church.

The Church

General

According to the Scriptures, the Church of Christ is the Body of Christ (Eph. 1:22-23; 1 Cor. 12; Rom. 12:4-5). As in this body, as in His human body before His crucifixion, the will of God is done on earth (Heb. 10:8-9). In the church this work is continued. There is the One Body, the universal church head, the local church, or Christ's Body [which is found] in any particular community. Locally speaking, the Church of Christ is composed of persons who have been born again.

Severally

Wherever two or three persons can be gathered together in one place, who have been born again, and been baptized, a Church may be organized.

Avowals of Belief

All persons seeking fellowship with the Church of Christ (Holiness) U.S.A. must believe the following statements:

1. In one God, "The Father, Son, and Holy Ghost."
2. That the Old and New Testament Scriptures are Divinely inspired.
3. That the above named Scriptures contain all truth necessary to Christian living.
4. That believers are to be sanctified, through faith in the Lord Jesus.
5. In the articles of faith in this Manual.

Another section on "special advices" has information on the role that women can play in leading worship.

Women

Whereas this policy may seem excessively restrictive to us today, at the time this validation of women's capability of teaching and leading might have seemed progressive.

Those women among us who evidence their gift and anointing of God to teach shall have the privilege to teach and conduct religious services in the Churches under the direction of the Pastor in charge. We do not license nor ordain women to preach, but under the Pastor's supervision she may teach and do general missionary work.

The following excerpts come from the section of the Manual on the local church.

Membership

1. All persons, after having declared their experience of salvation and their belief in the doctrines of the Church of Christ, and their willingness to submit to its government, shall be accepted as members of the church.

2. Persons coming to us from other churches, who have been baptized according to section (13) in articles of faith, shall not be rebaptized, unless by their request.

Officers

The Pastor

A Pastor is a person who, under the call of God and His people, has the oversight of a Local Church.

The Duties of a Pastor

One of the most important considerations for the actual conduct of worship is how a church configures ministry and what authority is given to what person. Defining some ministers by particular worship responsibilities goes back to the earliest centuries of church history.

1. To preach the Word.
2. Make pastoral visits, giving special care to the sick.
3. Baptize, and administer the Sacrament of the Lord's Supper.
4. Perform marriage ceremonies.
5. Reprove, rebuke, and exhort, with all long-suffering and doctrine.

These excerpts come from the Manual's fuller description of different categories of ministry. Notice the several different types of labels for ministers and ministry below and above.

The Ministry

Licensed Ministers

1. When there are those among us who feel called to the Ministry, they may be licensed by the Pastor of the Church, or the Presiding Bishop, provided they (1) have been proven one full year; (2) have passed the Course of Study for local preachers; (3) have been recommended by the Church of which they are members; (4) have been carefully examined by the Pastor and Deacons; (5) and shall have promised to pursue the Course of Study prescribed for candidates for Ordination.

2. A licensed Minister shall be vested with authority to preach the Word, and (only when acting as Pastor) to administer the Sacrament of Baptism, but not the Lord's Supper, in [his] own congregation, and to officiate at marriages where the laws of the state do not prohibit.

This denomination is following the lead of some other denominations (e.g., Methodist) which have a history of using unordained persons to serve as pastors of local congregations. Thus a congregation served by a licensed minister would not have to go without some important rites.

Ordained Elders

1. The Ordained Elders, only, are the recognized order of the Official Ministry. The Elder is to rule well in the Church, to preach the Word, to administer the Sacraments, and to Solemnize Matrimony, all in the name of the Great Head of the Church.

2. If a Licensed Minister has proven himself faithful for two years, in all things pertaining to the best interest of the Church and general work and has passed in the Course of Study prescribed for Ordination and is recommended by his Church or Pastor, he may be ordained by the laying on of the hands of the Presbytery.

While Jones used "ordinances," the denomination eventually adopted the term "sacraments."

The Evangelist

1. An Elder or a Licensed Minister who has completed at least one year of the Course of Study, and has been faithful to his Church and its cause, and is properly recommended, may be commissioned to do the work of an Evangelist.

2. The Evangelist shall make reports to the Convention in which he holds a membership. If the Evangelist has been Ordained, his authority shall be that of an Ordained Elder.

Although not clearly defined, evangelists seem to be preaching ministers without specific responsibility to one congregation only. They are thus free to travel to spread the Word and evangelize.

Source: *Manual of the History, Doctrine, Government, and Ritual of the Church of Christ (Holiness) U.S.A.*, 1st ed. (Norfolk, Va.: Guide Publishing Company, 1926), pp. 18, 21, 24-25, 33.

PART THREE

ASSISTING THE INVESTIGATION

Why Study Christ Temple's Worship?
Suggestions for Devotional Use

The following are suggestions for devotional use that correspond with specific sections of the book:

Describing the Community's Worship: Charles Price Jones and Christ Temple

- A critical part of Jones's early ministry involved an emphasis on healing. Consider the healing ministry of Jesus Christ under his anointing with the Holy Spirit. Bring specific Gospel stories to mind. Which of these images bring the most comfort to you with any disease or inward dis-ease you might be suffering?
- An important part of the preaching at Christ Temple was the offer of a new and richer infilling of the Holy Spirit. Pray, desire, and consider how a new movement of the Spirit — and the accompanying gifts of the Spirit (Gal. 5:22-23) — might bring healing to you.
- Imagine the physical and emotional toll the conflicts of the late 1890s must have had on Jones and his flock. Take time to put yourself into the shoes of one of these people. What would have been happening in your body, your mind, and your heart? Read slowly through the words of "I'm Happy with Jesus Alone." What words bring the most comfort to you?
- Consider the observation that "our churches are where we dip our tired bodies in cool springs of hope, where we retain our wholeness and humanity despite the blows of death. . . ." Think ahead to your church's next worship service. Ask God to bring to your mind someone who needs "cool springs of hope." What can you do to bring that refreshment to that person?

People and Artifacts

- In photographs, the people of Christ Temple reflect a quiet confidence as they look straight into the camera. Browse the Psalms and find three that contain statements of such confidence (e.g., "The Lord is my Shield" and "My trust is in the Lord"). Slowly repeat these statements out loud. Memorize two or three of the most reassuring verses.

Worship Setting and Space

- "Holiness unto the Lord" was the Bible verse written on the wall of Christ Temple. If you consider that you are a temple of the Lord (see 1 Cor. 3:16), what verse could you imagine God writing on the wall of your heart?

Descriptions of Worship

- Many of the firsthand accounts make references to passages of Scripture. Take your Bible and find all the passages referenced. What sort of passages appealed to those involved with Christ Temple?
- W. E. B. Du Bois characterized the "religion of the slave" as the preacher, the music, and the frenzy. Shift these terms a little to preaching, music, and deeply emotional times during worship. In which of these three do you most commonly sense the presence of God in worship? Or is it in sacraments, silence, the love found in church fellowship, or service to others?
- Notwithstanding whether speaking in tongues is the outward evidence of being filled with the Holy Spirit, the New Testament is quite clear that a Christian is to be a person of the Spirit. Go to the book of Acts and read it, looking for instances when a person was said to be "full of faith and the Holy Spirit." Cultivate a prayerful desire to become filled with the Holy Spirit.

Order of Service and Texts

- Memorize one of the songs by C. P. Jones, learning it as poetry only.
- Read through "The History of My Songs" by C. P. Jones. For each of the songs mentioned in the story and for which the lyrics are provided, imagine it on the lips of a character in a Bible story. Who could sing which song?
- Could the different scenes from Jones's "The History of My Songs" be portrayed visually? Sketch out a portrayal of his journey as told in this story.
- In the baptismal service, a candidate was asked to renounce "the world, the flesh, and the devil, [in order] to walk with Jesus." What would this same commitment mean for your life today?
- Read through the service for matrimony, circling every instance of the word "love." Are you surprised by how often it occurs? To what other actions (look for other verbs) do the couple commit themselves?

Sermons

- Jones's sermons seldom use personal anecdotes in their printed form. Instead, these sermons emphasize divine nature and activity. Read the sermons along with the book *Worship Comes to Its Senses* by Don E. Saliers. What affections toward God are brought out by these sermons? What passages in these sermons trigger in you a renewed love for God?

Theology of Worship Documents

- Despite the fact that C. P. Jones initiated reforms that resulted in conflict, one senses that he was genuinely troubled by disunity in the church. Pray and ask for discernment about how you might be bringing disunity to your congregation. Use 1 Corinthians 13 as a template for how you should act with respect to other Christians. As you read this, how are you convicted?

Why Study Christ Temple's Worship?
Discussion Questions for Small Groups

The following are discussion questions for each section of this book.

General Introduction and Timeline

- Do you think difficult times strengthen or weaken churches? What do you see as the most difficult challenges that Christ Temple and C. P. Jones faced?
- It has often been said that Sunday morning worship is the most racially segregated time of the week. Possible responses to this assertion include "It's inevitable," "It's atrocious," and "It's useful." Which strikes you as the most Christian response? Is there another appropriate response?

Describing the Community's Worship: Charles Price Jones and Christ Temple

- What do you think it would have been like to experience the type of racism that C. P. Jones and members of Christ Temple experienced? How would that have shaped their hopes and desires for Sunday morning?
- How do you think that class and social standing shape how a congregation worships? Does this happen in all congregations?
- What do you think was the most disruptive reform that C. P. Jones brought to Mt. Helm Baptist Church? Why was it the most disruptive?
- Do you think that forms of Christianity which emphasize personal experience create a context in which people are always seeking a new or deeper experience? Why or why not?
- Why do you think C. P. Jones tried to shift Mt. Helm Baptist Church into being more scriptural in its name and practices but resisted being persuaded on the same point by one of his closest ministerial allies, Charles Mason, when the latter had adopted Pentecostalism?

People and Artifacts

- Could age have played into C. P. Jones's style of pastoral leadership and into his spiritual hungers in the 1890s and early 1900s? (Jones turned thirty in 1895.) If so, how?

- Some of the main things which Jones published were new collections of songs. Why do promoting new music and spreading a new religious movement go hand in hand?

Worship Setting and Space

- Can looking at the front of a congregation's worship space tell you what it believes is most important in worship? What does the front of your congregation's space tell you?
- Why do you think the congregation that broke away from Mt. Helm Baptist Church ended up using biblical words for itself associated with God's dwelling or habitation (i.e., "tabernacle" and "temple")?
- How might a congregation's building location within a city be important?

Descriptions of Worship

- Which of the pastoral acts by C. P. Jones do you consider to be the most important? Which do you think was the most controversial? Why?
- Do you think those who followed C. P. Jones took his teaching to conclusions he did not intend?
- In the general description of African-American worship of the period, W. E. B. Du Bois highlights three things that characterized black worship: the preacher, the music, and the frenzy. Which of these three was most critical at Christ Temple? Why?
- "Charles Mason's View on the Tensions over Pentecostalism" and "C. P. Jones's View on the Tensions over Pentecostalism" show the different opinions of Jones and his former ally, Mason, about Pentecostalism. What was the heart of the disagreement between the two men? In what ways were their broader concerns similar? In what ways was Mason's becoming Pentecostal in line with what he and Jones had taught about the "higher life" of the Holiness movement?

Order of Service and Texts

- Many of Jones's songs focus specifically on Jesus Christ. What is the upside of having such a focus in worship? Is it possible to be too closely focused on Jesus Christ in worship devotion? Did you find much emphasis on God the Father and the Holy Spirit as recipients of worship in the material from Christ Temple?
- C. P. Jones had his most prolific times as a songwriter during the most turbulent times in his ministry. Is there a connection?
- Do you think a worship tradition can be fervent and passionate in its worship and still use written worship texts and prayers? Why or why not?

- In looking at the texts eventually published for some services, do you find it surprising that some of the texts reflect the influence of the African Methodist Episcopal Church (in their emphasis on marriage) and some more closely reflect a Baptist background (in their emphasis on baptism and the Lord's Supper)?

Sermons

- How do you think the experience of listening to C. P. Jones preach in person was different from reading the text of one of his sermons?
- A recurring feature of many complaints against ecstatic forms of Christianity is that the main participants have been "deluded women and irresponsible children." Why do you think that has been a common indictment?
- What are the main features of Jones's description of the roles of Jesus Christ and the Holy Spirit in salvation?

Theology of Worship Documents

- Is there any irony in Jones's beyond-denominationalism approach creating a congregation that ends up being the mother church for a new denomination? Was it avoidable? Was it inevitable?
- Certain clear theological commitments and distinctive practices characterized C. P. Jones and Christ Temple (e.g., sanctification and faith healing). That is common for new movements of revitalization. How do you think those commitments and practices fared over time? Did they remain important for later generations? Does it make any difference whether or not they did?

Polity Documents

- Did the later organizational documents for Jones's denomination capture the spirit of his early ministry in Jackson?

Why Study Christ Temple's Worship? A Guide for Different Disciplines and Areas of Interest

Christianity

If you are interested in Christianity as a religion generally, then Christ Temple is helpful for understanding the following:

- distinctive African-American forms of worship and the diversity therein;
- the nature of Christian devotional attachment to Jesus;
- strands of Christian thought that eschew tradition and seek to re-establish New Testament Christianity as their main goal;
- the popularity of evangelical and charismatic Christianity;
- possible relationships between religion and culture.

Here are discussion questions based on these general religious issues:

- How would you say Christ Temple handled its roots in the religion of slaves as its African-American members sought social and economic advancement? Was it successful, unsuccessful, or were the results mixed?
- What best exemplifies these Christians' attachment to Jesus Christ? Why is C. P. Jones's devotion so focused upon Christ and not the other Persons of Christianity's Triune God?
- What drives the desire to renew Christianity by a "back-to-the-Bible-only" approach? Are there parallel phenomena in other religions?
- To what would you attribute the numeric success of C. P. Jones's ministry?
- What aspects of church life most enabled the members of Christ Temple to handle the oppression of Jim Crow racism?

Christian Worship

If you are interested in worship generally, then Christ Temple is helpful for understanding the following:

- how a congregation might juggle both contextual and countercultural elements in finding appropriate ways of worship for itself;
- the common Protestant approach whereby music and preaching overshadow administration of baptism and the Lord's Supper;

- liturgical piety that is affect-based yet seeks to resist excessive emotionalism or ecstatic expression.

Here are discussion questions based on these general worship issues:

- At what points was Christ Temple adapting to its cultural context and at what points was it evidencing a stand against it?
- The congregation's names (i.e., "tabernacle" and "temple") are biblical terms with strong allusions to dwelling places for God's presence. In which of the following do you suspect that this congregation most expected to experience God's presence in worship: their own fellowship, preaching, music, sacraments/ordinances, or the building itself?
- Is it inevitable that forms of Christianity that emphasize heartwarming experiences in individual salvation will also seek heartwarming experiences in corporate worship? Did Christ Temple successfully negotiate touching the heart in worship while avoiding excesses?

Music

If you are interested in music, then Christ Temple is helpful for understanding the following:

- the work of C. P. Jones as one of the early, prolific composers of Black Gospel music;
- the interaction between context and creativity in the process of composition, as seen in the social and ecclesiastical settings for Jones's compositions;
- the focus on Jesus Christ as a standard feature of Black Gospel music.

Here are discussion questions based on these music issues:

- Within gospel music, how is the work of Jones exemplary for the genre as a whole?
- Is it surprising that the period of Jones's most prolific composing output was also his period of intense spiritual experiences, vibrant public ministry, and tumultuous church politics? Why do you think he was so productive during this time?
- Friend, Protector, Liberator. Which of the three images for Christ do you think is predominant in the lyrics written by Jones?

Spirituality

If you are interested in spirituality, then Christ Temple is helpful for understanding the following:

- the nature of intense devotional piety directed toward Jesus Christ;
- the role of corporate worship and ritual in maintaining positive spirituality in the midst of a hostile existence;

- the demonstration of a pastor's desire to move people beyond mere church affiliation;
- various kinds of ecstatic ritual expression.

Here are discussion questions based on these spirituality issues:
- Is there something about Jesus Christ, as compared to the other two Persons of the Triune God, which makes possible affect-based devotional piety? If so, what? Why did contemplating Jesus Christ stimulate such intensity in C. P. Jones?
- In what ways did the worship of Christ Temple allow its members to negotiate life in an antagonistic social environment?
- What allows church members to be satisfied with nominal membership? How did C. P. Jones attack this sentiment? Why might he have been ferocious in his denunciations of "secret societies" to which his members belonged?
- Is expressing ecstasy in ritual a learned behavior, or is it spontaneous? Which of these options best explains the early Pentecostal experience of Charles Mason?

Church History

If you are interested in church history, then Christ Temple is helpful for understanding the following:
- the Holiness movement as the backdrop for the rise of Pentecostalism;
- the way in which an originally iconoclastic renewal movement can become its own institution;
- the ways in which Christian revitalization movements can connect people across denominational lines.

Here are discussion questions based on these church history issues:
- What aspects of the Holiness movement's doctrines and practices might have led Charles Mason to seek a Pentecostal experience? Why do you think C. P. Jones might have rejected the same?
- Could C. P. Jones's original vision of getting beyond denominationalism be sustained? Was it a reasonable dream?
- In what ways did the Holiness movement — and, in more recent times, the Charismatic movement — make Christians' denominational identity less important? Is the offer of a common experience the thing that crosses denominational lines?

Glossary

Baptism of/with the Holy Spirit/Ghost   A term used by both the Holiness movement and early Pentecostalism, based on Acts 1:5, to describe a deeper Christian experience associated with an infilling of the Holy Spirit. The two movements differ on what the outward evidence of the experience should be.

Black Gospel music   A sub-genre of gospel music associated with and coming from African-American churches. Characterized by strong vocals and lyrics that often reference personal and communal experience and beliefs, Black Gospel music reflects not only an evangelical sensibility but also a perspective influenced by the status of blacks in America.

Christ Tabernacle   The early name for the congregation that would eventually be known as Christ Temple.

Evangelical faith   A dominant form of Christianity found in the United States, usually including some combination of these characteristics: a strong reliance upon the Bible as authoritative, a seeking after salvation based on the work of Christ, a commitment to engaging in evangelism and missions to others, and an assumption that faith in Christ leads to a transformed life.

Gospel music   See Black Gospel music.

Higher life   A term from the Holiness movement that was a shorthand way of referring to the more intense, thorough discipleship that resulted from the inward sanctifying work of the Spirit of Jesus Christ subsequent to one's initial experience of salvation.

Holiness convention   As used in this volume, the name for the annual regional meetings hosted by Christ Temple at which Christian renewal, especially holiness or sanctification, was promoted.

Holiness movement   A Christian movement arising in the nineteenth century, ultimately derived from the teachings of John Wesley and his Methodists. It sought to promote as its chief tenet the opportunity for people already saved as Christians to have a second experience called "sanctification" (among other possible terms). This cleansing work by the Holy Spirit empowered Christians to begin to live out the holiness of God.

Invitation   An appeal at the end of a worship service, especially to come be saved or confess one's faith in Christ.

Jim Crow   A term referring to the state existing when laws began to be passed in the late nineteenth century requiring separation of races in public venues. While sometimes portrayed as providing a "separate but equal" situation, in actuality it led to black Americans suffering economic, educational, and social disadvantages. Thus the term can also refer to the systemic racism present at that time.

Landmarkism   A kind of Baptist doctrine which developed and spread among whites and blacks in the nineteenth century. The doctrine emphasized the unique authenticity and legitimacy of Baptist churches, including succession to the first-century apostolic period; this involved the rejection of the validity of other churches. Thus the doctrine includes-dthe rejection of baptisms and ordinations performed in other churches.

Mt. Helm Baptist Church   The original church in Jackson, Mississippi, which called C. P. Jones as pastor. It was a large, influential black congregation in the city and state. Christ Temple arose out of a schism within this church.

Parsonage   A church-supplied home for a pastor.

Pentecostal/Pentecostalism   A type of Christianity, from the early 20th century, so named because its adherents see themselves as having recovered the power and phenomena of the original Pentecost. Key emphases include a distinct infilling of the Holy Spirit, an experience normally called "baptism in the Holy Spirit" after the terminology of the biblical book Acts, and the evidence of the Holy Spirit by speaking in tongues. Pentecostals also affirm the manifestation of other spiritual gifts as listed in Scripture.

Reconstruction   The period after the Civil War (1861-1865) during which economic, civic, and social structures were rebuilt or reformed in the American South. The status and rights of newly-freed slaves were major concerns.

Restoration Movement   A movement arising out of American religious revivals in the early part of the nineteenth century which sought to achieve Christian unity by finding common agreement on the Bible and avoiding common sources of division such as creeds, ecclesiastical traditions, and names of human origins. Denominations which arose out of this movement include the Disciples of Christ, the Churches of Christ, and the Christian Church. Although C. P. Jones shared similar opinions, his ministry was not directly connected with this movement.

Sanctification   A second experience of salvation subsequent to justification. Whereas justification deals with forgiveness of sins (what God does for us), sanctification involves an inward transformation by which God deals with our inclination to sin or with the power of sin (what God does in us). Detractors often accused sanctification proponents of promising "sinless perfection," which was a false charge with respect to C. P. Jones.

Speaking in tongues   As used in this volume, this term refers to speech given supernaturally by the Holy Spirit which sounds unintelligible to the human ear. Speaking in tongues is also known as glossolalia, after the Greek word in the New Testament for tongues or languages. Acts and First Corinthians are important scriptures for those who emphasize the experience.

Tongues   See Speaking in tongues.

Suggestions for Further Study

Read these books and articles:

Abbington, James, ed. *Readings in African American Church Music and Worship.* Chicago: GIA Publications, Inc., 2001

Abbington, James, Jr. "Bishop Charles Price Jones (1865-1949)." *The African American Pulpit* 9, no. 1 (Winter 2005-2006): 23-27.

Blumhofer, Edith L. " 'Jesus Only': The Ministry of Charles Price Jones." *Assemblies of God Heritage* 7 (Spring 1987): 14-15.

Burgess, Stanley M., and Eduard M. Van Der Maas, eds. *The New International Dictionary of Pentecostal and Charismatic Movements.* Revised and expanded edition. Grand Rapids: Zondervan, 2002.

Costen, Melva Wilson. *African American Christian Worship.* 2nd ed. Nashville: Abingdon Press, 2007.

Costen, Melva Wilson, and Darius Leander Swann, eds. *The Black Christian Worship Experience.* Revised and enlarged edition. Black Church Scholars Series, vol. IV. Atlanta: ITC Press, 1992.

Daniels, David Douglas. "The Cultural Renewal of Slave Religion: Charles Price Jones and the Emergence of the Holiness Movement in Mississippi." Ph.D. dissertation, Union Theological Seminary, 1992.

Dupree, Sherry Sherrod. *African-American Holiness Pentecostal Movement: An Annotated Bibliography.* New York: Garland Publishing, Inc., 1996.

Giggie, John M. *After Redemption: Jim Crow and the Transformation of African American Religion in the Delta, 1875-1915.* New York: Oxford University Press, 2008.

Irvin, Dale T. "Charles Price Jones: Image of Holiness." In *Portraits of a Generation: Early Pentecostal Leaders.* Edited by James R. Goff Jr. and Grant Wacker. Fayetteville: University of Arkansas Press, 2002.

Jones, Charles Edwin. *The Wesleyan Holiness Movement: A Comprehensive Guide.* Lanham, Md.: Scarecrow Press, 2005.

Sanders, Cheryl J. *Saints in Exile: The Holiness-Pentecostal Experience in African American Religion and Culture.* New York: Oxford University Press, 1996.

Sidwell, Mark. "Charles Price Jones." In *Free Indeed: Heroes of Black Christian History*. Greenville, S.C.: Bob Jones University Press, 2001.

Spencer, Jon Michael. "The Hymnody of Charles Price Jones and the Church of Christ (Holiness) U.S.A." *Black Sacred Music: A Journal of Theomusicology* 4 (1990): 14-29.

Wacker, Grant A. "Travail of a Broken Family: Radical Evangelical Responses to the Emergence of Pentecostalism in America, 1906-16." In *Pentecostal Currents in American Protestantism*. Edited by Edith L. Blumhofer, Russell P. Spittler, and Grant A. Wacker. Urbana and Chicago: University of Illinois Press, 1999.

The denominational histories produced by Church of Christ (Holiness) U.S.A. members also provide useful information on Charles Price Jones and his original congregation in Jackson. See these volumes:

Castilla, Willenham. *Moving Forward on God's Highway: A Textbook History of the Church of Christ (Holiness) U.S.A.* Bloomington, Ind.: AuthorHouse, 2007.

Cobbins, Otho B., ed. *History of Church of Christ (Holiness) U.S.A., 1895-1965.* New York: Vantage Press, 1966.

Jefferson, Anita Bingham, ed. *Excellence Comes with Great Labor: Writings of Bishop Charles Price Jones, 1865-1949.* 2009.

Visit these Web sites:

Church of Christ (Holiness) U.S.A.: *http://www.cochusa.org*

> This link will take you to the denominational Web site, where you can find more information on the denomination Jones started.

The Society for Pentecostal Studies: *http://sps-usa.org*

> The resources page of this organization's Web site contains links that will help you find more information on the Holiness movement and early Pentecostalism.

The Wesley Center for Applied Theology: *http://wesley.nnu.edu*

> Here you can find many links to primary material derived from the history of the broader Holiness movement.

Behind the Veil: Documenting African American Life in the Jim Crow South:
  http://library.duke.edu/digitalcollections/behindtheveil

  Go to the "Behind the Veil" Web site to hear a selection of one hundred recorded oral history interviews chronicling African-American life during the age of legal segregation in the American South starting in the 1890s.

Listen to this music:

Two CDs produced by the Church of Christ (Holiness) U.S.A. contain texts written by Jones and sung by a choir to new musical arrangements. Although it's difficult to determine what music would have sounded like in the original Christ Temple at the beginning of the twentieth century, these recordings at least show the ongoing vitality of Jones's lyrics. The two CDs are *COCHUSA Live* and *COCHUSA Live II*.

Visit a Church of Christ (Holiness) U.S.A. church:

A visit to a Church of Christ (Holiness) U.S.A. congregation will allow you to see the ongoing legacy of C. P. Jones and his ministry at Christ Temple. Lists of churches by region are available by following the link for COCHUSA dioceses at http://www.cochusa.org/about-cochusa/.

Works Cited

The Apostolic Faith 1, no. 6 (February-March 1907): 7.

The Apostolic Faith 1, no. 7 (April 1907): 3.

The Apostolic Faith 1, no. 12 (January 1908): 4.

Burgess, Stanley M., and Eduard M. Van Der Maas, eds. *The New International Dictionary of Pentecostal and Charismatic Movements.* Revised and expanded ed. Grand Rapids: Zondervan, 2002.

Cobbins, Otho B., ed. *History of Church of Christ (Holiness) U.S.A., 1895-1965.* New York: Vantage Press, 1966.

Costen, Melva Wilson. *African American Christian Worship.* 2nd ed. Nashville: Abingdon Press, 2007.

Crawford, Isaiah W., and Patrick H. Thompson. *Multum in Parvo: An Authenticated History of Progressive Negroes in Pleasing and Graphic Biographical Style.* Natchez, Miss.: Consumers Printing Co., 1912.

Daniel, Vattel Elbert. "Ritual and Stratification in Chicago Negro Churches." *American Sociological Review* 7 (1942): 352-61.

Daniels, David Douglas. "The Cultural Renewal of Slave Religion: Charles Price Jones and the Emergence of the Holiness Movement in Mississippi." Ph.D. dissertation, Union Theological Seminary, 1992.

Dayton, Donald. "The Rise of the Evangelical Healing Movement in Nineteenth-Century America." *Pneuma* 4, no. 1 (1982): 1-18.

———. *Theological Roots of Pentecostalism.* Peabody, Mass.: Hendrickson, 1987.

Dieter, Melvin E. *The Holiness Revival of the Nineteenth Century.* 2nd ed. Lanham, Md.: Scarecrow Press, 1996.

Du Bois, W. E. B. *The Souls of Black Folk: Essays and Sketches.* Chicago: McClurg, 1904.

Gatewood, Willard B., Jr. "Aristocrats of Color South and North: The Black Elite, 1880-1920." *The Journal of Southern History* 54, no. 1 (1988): 3-20.

Harrison, Alferdteen. *The Farish Street Historic District: Memories, Perceptions, and Developmental Alternatives.* Jackson, Miss.: Jackson State University, Institute for the Study of History, Life, and Culture of Black People, 1984.

Hatch, Nathan O. *The Democratization of American Christianity.* New Haven: Yale University Press, 1989.

Irvin, Dale T. "Charles Price Jones: Image of Holiness." In *Portraits of a Generation: Early Pentecostal Leaders.* Edited by James R. Goff Jr. and Grant Wacker. Fayetteville: University of Arkansas Press, 2002.

Jones, Charles P. *An Appeal to the Sons of Africa.* Jackson, Miss.: National Publishing Board, Church of Christ (Holiness), 2000.

———. *The Gift of the Holy Spirit in the Book of Acts.* Jackson, Miss.: National Publishing Board, Church of Christ (Holiness), 1996.

———. *Jesus Only, Nos. 1 and 2 Combined.* Bogalusa, La.: R. C. Cook for the National Publishing Board of the Church of Christ (Holiness), 1935.

———. "Our Weekly Sermon: Abstinence from Evil." *Truth* 8 (17 September 1903): 2.

———. *Sermons of Life and Power.* Jackson, Miss.: Truth Publishing Co., 1913; reprint edition, National Publishing Board, Church of Christ (Holiness) U.S.A., 2004.

Jones, Raymond Julius. "Comparative Study of Religious Cult Behavior among Negroes." Dissertation, Graduate School for the Division of the Social Sciences, Howard University, 1939.

Manual of the History, Doctrine, Government, and Ritual of the Church of Christ (Holiness) U.S.A., 1926. Norfolk, Va.: Guide Publishing Company, 1926.

Mason, Mary, comp. *The History and Life Work of Elder C. H. Mason and His Co-Laborers.* Memphis, Tenn.: Church of God in Christ, 1924; reprint, 1987.

McCain, William D. *The Story of Jackson: A History of the Capital of Mississippi, 1821-1951.* Jackson, Miss.: J. F. Hyer, 1953.

McMillen, Neil R. *Dark Journey: Black Mississippians in the Age of Jim Crow.* Champaign: University of Illinois Press, 1989.

Mitchell, Henry. *This Far by Faith: American Black Worship and Its African Roots.* Washington: National Office for Black Catholics, 1977.

Montgomery, William E. *Under Their Own Vine and Fig Tree: The African-American Church in the South, 1865-1900.* Baton Rouge: Louisiana State University Press, 2000.

Sidwell, Mark. *Free Indeed: Heroes of Black Christian History.* Greenville, S.C.: Bob Jones University Press, 2001.

Spencer, Jon M. "The Hymnody of Charles Price Jones and the Church of Christ (Holiness) U.S.A." *Black Sacred Music: A Journal of Theomusicology* 4, no. 2 (1990).

———. *Protest and Praise: Sacred Music of Black Religion.* Minneapolis: Fortress Press, 1990.

Thompson, Patrick H. *The History of Negro Baptists in Mississippi.* Jackson, Miss.: R. W. Bailey Print Co., 1898.

Truth 7 (19 March 1903): 26.

Wharton, Vernon Lane. *The Negro in Mississippi: 1865-1890.* Reprint ed. New York: Harper & Row, 1965.

Williams, Lee E. *Mt. Helm Baptist Church, 1835-1988: The Parade of Pastors, 1864-1988.* Jackson, Miss.: Williams, 1988.

Wright, Richard. *12 Million Black Voices: A Folk History of the Negro in the United States.* New York: Viking Press, 1941.

Index